Shanghai Cooperation Organisation
Reconnect ~ Rejuvenate

Shanghai Cooperation Organisation
Reconnect ~ Rejuvenate

Edited by

Athar Zafar

SCO Study Centre
Indian Council of World Affairs
Sapru House
2024

KW Publishers Pvt Ltd
New Delhi

Indian Council of World Affairs
New Delhi

ISBN 978-81-973214-9-8 Hardback

Published in India by Kalpana Shukla

KW Publishers Pvt Ltd
4676/21, First Floor, Ansari Road
Daryaganj, New Delhi 110 002
Phone: +91 11 43528107
Marketing: kw@kwpub.in
Editorial: production@kwpub.in
Website: www.kwpub.in

Printed and bound in India

Contents

Foreword

The Shanghai Cooperation Organisation (SCO) seeks to promote regional collaboration through a consensus-building approach.

India became a member of the SCO in 2017 and Prime Minister Narendra Modi, speaking at the 18th SCO Summit in 2018, outlined India's approach to its engagement with the SCO as the 'SECURE' concept—Security, Economic cooperation, Culture, Unity, Respect for sovereignty and territorial integrity and Environment. India views Central Asia, which is the focal area of the SCO, as its extended neighbourhood. It seeks to rekindle its civilisational relationship with this crucial region and forge cooperation in fields like energy, technology and sustainable development. Connectivity has been identified as a primary area for greater economic cooperation in the SCO.

India was the Chair of the SCO for the period 2022-23. During its presidency, India's effort was to improve connectivity at all levels, including in the field of knowledge sharing. In this context, the Indian Council of World Affairs organised an 'International Conference on Shanghai Cooperation Organisation: Reconnect ~ Rejuvenate' in March 2023, inviting representatives/experts from SCO member states as well as from observer and dialogue partner countries. The present publication is a collection of papers/presentations made by the experts at this conference. It is a compendium of views on the SCO and regional developments from diverse perspectives. The papers contain suggestions and policy recommendations for the further strengthening of cooperation among the SCO countries.

I am confident that this publication will be useful for scholars and diplomats alike, regarding pathways for further strengthening cooperation within the SCO.

Amb. **Vijay Thakur Singh**
Director General, ICWA

Contributors

Mr. Zhumabek Sarabekov is Expert and Head of the Eurasian Studies Program of the Institute of World Economy and Politics (IWEP) under the N. Nazarbayev Foundation, Astana, Kazakhstan. He did his graduation (2007-2011) as well as post-graduation (2011-2013) from the Faculty of International Relations, Al-Farabi Kazakh National University. He also attended the academic programme on "Modern approaches to social and humanitarian studies in Europe" from Leiden University, the Netherlands, in 2013. Since 2013, he has been working as Foreign Policy Expert at the IWEP. His areas of research include the politics and geoeconomics of Central Asia and the South Caucasus regions. He has more than 100 publications in various scientific and socio-political journals to his credit.

Dr. Deng Hao is Secretary General of China Center for SCO studies; Senior Research Fellow at the China Institute of International Studies and Executive Editor of the SCO Blue Book. From 1998 till 2001, he worked as Senior Research Fellow at the China Institute of International Studies and Director of the Department for European-Central Asian Studies. He was appointed as the first Secretary at the Head of Political Section of the Chinese Embassy in Turkmenistan from 2002-2006 and as the Head of Political Section of the Chinese Embassy in Kazakhstan during 2006-2008. He has served as the Political Counsellor of the Chinese Embassy in Kyrgyzstan from 2009-2013 and of the Chinese Embassy in Georgia from 2013-2015.

Ms. Altynai Kanatbekovna Aliiaskarova is a Researcher at the National Institute for Strategic Studies of the Kyrgyz Republic, Bishkek, Kyrgyzstan, since 2022. She did her graduation in Linguistics from Bishkek, Kyrgyzstan

(2014-2018) and Master of Law from East China Normal University (the School of Advanced International and Area Studies), Shanghai, China (2018-2021). She is also a postgraduate from Bishkek State University. From 2021-2022, Ms. Altynai served as Head Specialist of the 'One Belt-One Road' Research Centre at Kyrgyz National University, which is named after Jusup Balasagyn (Kyrgyz-Chinese Faculty). In 2021, she worked as an engineer at the Department of State Statistics and Department of Small and Medium Business Statistics in Bishkek city.

Ms. Ume Farwa is a Research Associate at the Institute of Strategic Studies Islamabad (ISSI), Islamabad, Pakistan. Her area of research includes multilateralism in Indian foreign policy, Maldives and Bhutan. She has an M.Phil. in International Relations from the National University of Modern Languages. She is a gold medalist in Masters in International Relations from NUML. She has co-edited a book, "CPEC: A Game Changer", which is a joint venture of Pakistani and Chinese scholars. In the capacity of the sub-editor of the ISSI journal, she has edited research papers and manuscripts on diverse topics, such as international relations, history, public policy, governance and strategic studies. Currently, she is working on alternative knowledge perspectives in IR – termed as 'Global IR' – particularly, on the Sufi theory of international relations.

Professor Saidmurodov Lyutfillo is Director, Department of Comparative Economic Research, Institute of Economics and Demography, National Academy of Sciences of Tajikistan. He completed doctorate (Doctor of Economic Sciences) in Economics and Diploma from the Institute of Economic Researches, Ministry of Economy and Trade, Dushanbe, Tajikistan, from 2002-2005. Prof. Saidmurodov has also completed an advanced degree in Economics and Diploma from Moscow State University, Moscow, Russian Federation. He has previously worked as Director at the Institute of Economics and Demography, Academy of Sciences of the Republic of Tajikistan, from April 2015-2020. Prof. Saidmurodov was recently honoured as the Academician of the International Academy of Engineering (2018). He was also presented with the Governmental Medal "For Services" (2004).

Mr. Batyr Tursunov is Deputy Director, International Institute of Central Asia, Tashkent, Uzbekistan, since November 2022. He graduated from the Tashkent State Institute of Oriental Studies and completed his postgraduate studies at the Institute of Philosophy and Law of the Academy of Sciences of the Republic of Uzbekistan. Mr. Batyr has served as Deputy Director, Institute for Strategic and Inter-Regional Studies under the President of the Republic of Uzbekistan (2017-2019) and as Minister-Counsellor, Embassy of the Republic of Uzbekistan and Permanent Representative of the Republic of Uzbekistan to the SCO Secretariat (2019-2022). From March 2022 to November 2022, he was appointed the Chief Consultant of the Executive Office of the Presidential Administration of the Republic of Uzbekistan.

Dr. Makarov Oleg Sergeevich is serving as Director, Belarusian Institute for Strategic Studies, Minsk, Belarus. He is a Doctor of Law and Associate Professor. He graduated from the Faculty of Law of Grodno State University and presented his dissertation at the Institute of State and Law of the Russian Academy of Sciences, with a degree in Information Law. Dr. Makarov is one of the developers of the concept of information security of Belarus, the strategy of information security of the CIS member states and model laws of the CIS member states "on information, informatisation and information security". Previously, he led the Information and Analytical Department of the State Secretariat of the Security Council of Belarus. His sphere of interests and research are international law, information security, theory of ensuring the national security of Belarus and analytics. Dr. Makarov is the author of numerous scientific publications, including publications abroad as well as monographs and textbooks.

Ms. Soyolgerel Nyamjav is Head of the International Security Studies Centre and Senior Research Fellow at the Institute for Strategic Studies, Mongolia, since August 2009. From 2001-2005, she worked as a full-time lecturer at the Mongolian National University of Education. She was awarded the Mongolian 'Medal of Honour Labour' and a medal for taking part in the NATO-led operation, 'Resolute Support', in Afghanistan, in 2017. She also received "The Best Junior" gold medal from the Mongolian Youth Federation in 2012. Ms. Soyolgerel received training as Asia Studies Visiting Fellow at the East-West Centre in Washington from May 2018 - August 2018 and also attended a programme on Advanced Security Cooperation in the Asia-Pacific Centre for Security Studies in Hawaii, USA (May, 2017). She visited Turkey for KATIP, the Turkish Culture and Diplomacy Training Programme, from December 2014 to August 2015.

Dr. Gohar Iskandaryan is Head of the Department of Iranian Studies, Institute of Oriental Studies, National Academy of Sciences, Yerevan,

Armenia. She is a leading researcher and the author of three monographs - 'Iran-US Relations, 1942-1960', 'Armenian-Iranian Relations since the Independence of Armenia' and 'Political Structure of IRI' - and has more than 35 academic articles to her credit. Since 2012, she has been teaching at the Yerevan State University in the Department of History and Oriental Studies. Dr. Iskandaryan has participated in more than 40 international conferences and has organised three international conferences on Iran-Armenian relations. She is the editor-in-chief of three collective volumes. She provides policy advice to the Ministry of Foreign Affairs, the Parliament and the National Security Council of Armenia and often, public comments through the media.

H. E. Abdulrahman Al Gaoud is Ambassador of the Kingdom of Bahrain to India. He holds a Bachelor's Degree in Aviation from Oxford, UK and a Master's Degree in Aviation and Air Transport. In 2002, he was promoted to the position of Under Secretary of Civil Aviation Affairs. He served as the chairman of the Executive Committee and a board member of Gulf Air until December 2005 and as a board member of Gulf Aircraft Maintenance Company (GAMCO) and Gulf Helicopters Company. Ambassador Abdulrahman has made multiple contributions to the Arab Civil Aviation Authority and the field of air transport. He was honoured in Dubai, UAE, in recognition of his significant role, services, contributions and achievements in the civil aviation sector in the Kingdom of Bahrain in particular and the Gulf region's international air transport sector.

Dr. Ahmed Kandil is Head of International Affairs Unit and Head of Energy Studies Program, Al-Ahram Center for Political and Strategic Studies (ACPSS), Cairo, Egypt. He completed his B.Sc. in Political Science from Cairo University in 1995 and his MA in International Relations from the International University of Japan. He holds a Ph.D. in Philosophy of International Relations from Sophia University (Tokyo). He is a Fellow of the National Defence College, Nasser Higher Military Academy in Cairo. He received this fellowship with distinction in 2018 and was honoured by the Egyptian Defence Minister. He was the editor-in-chief of the "Marsad Al-Taqa" or "Energy Monitor" periodical. He specialises in the Eastern Mediterranean region, East Asia and the Middle East. Dr. Kandil currently focuses on the issues of security and energy partnerships in the Eastern Mediterranean region as well as those of climate change and energy.

Mr. Lim Menghour is Director of Mekong Centre for Strategic Studies (MCSS) of the Asian Vision Institute (AVI), Phnom Penh, Cambodia, since October 2022. He has completed his Master's degree (M.Sc.) in International Relations from the University of Bristol and has done his graduation in International Studies at the Department of International Studies (DIS), Institute of Foreign Languages (IFL), Royal University of Phnom Penh (RUPP). Mr. Lim is also a Bachelor of Arts in Economic Science, specialising in Enterprise Management, from the Royal University of Law and Economics (RULE). From July 2019 – September 2022, he served as Deputy Director of MCSS of the AVI. Previously, from November 2018 – February 2020, he was a lecturer at the Department of International Studies, IFL, RUPP. He has authored several research papers and book chapters and has been awarded various research grants.

H. E. Jasem Al-Najem is Ambassador of the State of Kuwait to the Republic of India. Ambassador Jasem holds a Bachelor's degree in Political Science from Kuwait University. He was appointed to the Permanent Mission of the State of Kuwait to the United Nations, in New York, in 2004. Amb. Najem has participated in many ministerial meetings while he was a member of this mission, in the period 2004-2009. He was promoted as Counsellor in 2007. Amb. Najem has served as Deputy Head of Mission in Beirut (2009-2013) and in Ankara (2013-14). He has served as Ambassador of the State of Kuwait to the United Republic of Tanzania (2015-2018), the Republic of India (since October 2018) and Nepal (since August 2019), with residence in New Delhi.

Dr. Aly Shameem is Assistant Professor at Maldives National University, Male, Maldives. He is a member of the Advisory Committee of Dhivehi Bahuge Academy (Regulator & Promoter of National and Official Languages, Dhivehi). He completed his post-graduation from Dalhousie University, Canada, in 1995 and Ph.D. from the International Global Change Institute, University of Waikato, New Zealand, in 2006. He served as Chairperson, Advisory Committee of Faculty of Arts, Maldives National University (2018–2021). From August 2015-July 2020, he served as President/Chairman, Civil Service Commission of Maldives and as Member/Commissioner, Judicial Service Commission. He is a founding member of the South Asia Network of Public Administration (Bangladesh). His research interests include public administration, governance, public management, climate politics and policy, ocean politics and policy, islands diplomacy, regional security, multilateral politics and policy, human rights and democracy.

Dr. Ebtesam Alteneiji is Director of Community Services Sector, Emirates Center for Strategic Studies and Research (ECSSR), Abu Dhabi, United Arab Emirates. She is also a faculty member at the Government and Society Department at the United Arab Emirates University. Before joining ECSSR in July 2021, Dr. Alteneiji served as the Director of UAE University Center for Public Policy and Leadership. She has received both a Ph.D. in Organisational Leadership and Consulting and an M.A. in Leadership Studies from the University of San Diego, USA. Her research is focused on studying inter-generational value changes in fast changing societies, such as the case in the UAE and cultural changes in general.

Ms. Yasoja Gunasekara is Additional Secretary, Bilateral Affairs (East), Ministry of Foreign Affairs, Colombo, Sri Lanka. She is a career diplomat with over 25 years of experience in the Ministry of Foreign Affairs and diplomatic missions of Sri Lanka. Prior to her assignment as Additional Secretary/Bilateral Affairs-East, she served as Ambassador in Jakarta and as High Commissioner in Dhaka. She established the consulate in Guangzhou, China, in 2012 and was the first Consul General. She also served in Sri Lanka High Commission in New Delhi and in Permanent Representative of UN, New York where she covered 1st and 3rd Committees and assisted Sri Lanka Presidency of UN Review Conference on UN Programme of Action on Small Arms in July 2006, amongst other responsibilities. She has completed her Bachelor's degree in Law from Warwick University, in the UK and Masters in Foreign Affairs and Trade from Monash University, in Australia.

Introduction

A significant post-Cold War development in Eurasian regional diplomacy has been the establishment of the Shanghai Cooperation Organisation (SCO), in June 2001, as a forum for regional cooperation. The core values of the SCO are building mutual trust and a team approach to overcoming obstacles. Both regionalism and regional cooperation have been bolstered by it. With the dawn of the 21st century bringing with it a number of changes, this organisation is in a unique position to provide a narrative of cooperation and strengthen cooperative multilateralism. The world community aspires to a multipolar world, where various civilisations, cultures and political systems coexist and the SCO stands for this goal.

The SCO expanded its agenda to include economic integration, connectivity enhancement, digitalisation and other topics, after its initial phase of internal organisation and creation of mechanisms like the Secretariat and the Regional Anti-Terrorist Structure (RATS), which are based in Beijing, China and Tashkent, Uzbekistan, respectively.

The SCO seeks to contribute to the 'promotion of a new democratic, fair and rational political and economic international order'. Countries from different parts of the world are seeking to become SCO partners and contribute to its vision, given the vital role that it can play in enhancing coordination for regional and global stability. The induction of many countries, especially the Arab and Gulf countries, as dialogue partners in the SCO signifies the growing importance of this platform in different regions including the Middle East and underlines their desire to play a greater role in fostering inter-regional cooperation.

Anchored in the centrality of Eurasia, the SCO has the potential to lead the region for a reinvigorated and reformed multilateral system, especially of the UN. The SCO has also made contact with other important organisations, such as the United Nations (UN), Eurasian Economic Union (EUEA), Collective Security Treaty Organisation (CSTO) and Association of South-East Asian Nations (ASEAN).

As the SCO gains strength and widens its reach, the expectations from it as well as the challenges it faces are also growing. The SCO space and its surroundings are faced with traditional and non-traditional security challenges, which impact the region of Eurasia. The COVID-19 pandemic highlighted the close connection between economic development and security, including public health. Promoting disaster-resistant infrastructure is essential for lowering financial losses and enhancing community well-being during emergencies.

Being a Eurasian country, it is natural for India to be associated with any major Eurasia-focused initiative, including the SCO. The SCO was established in 2001 and India joined as an observer state in 2005. After over a decade of association, India was accorded its membership in 2017, which was supported by all the member countries. India chaired the SCO for 2022-23 and its approach to the chairmanship of the SCO was typified by its belief that 'the world is one family'. The Eurasian region can progress when it is geographically connected, economically integrated and politically predictable. The SCO members must work together to preserve and guarantee peace, security and stability in the area.

It is necessary to combat the insecurity brought on by terrorism, extremism and cyber threats since they obstruct peace and economic advancement. We, in the region, must confront and find a solution to the effects of the current state of affairs in Afghanistan. The SCO can be well-positioned politically, economically and logistically to contribute to Afghanistan's stabilisation efforts. Afghanistan has the enormous potential to serve as a 'roundabout' for regional connectivity, which could benefit the entire region. The efforts to help the Afghan people fulfill their basic needs and aspirations and provide them aid and humanitarian relief need to continue.

Maintaining the centrality of Central Asia, the SCO seeks to foster efficient collaboration in the areas of economics, technology, education, energy, transportation, tourism and environmental conservation. Creating comprehensive regional connectivity will help accomplish these goals. Reconnection is essential to revitalise the SCO space. Landlocked countries in the SCO family need easy access to oceans for trade and conducting scientific research. Many SCO members have a history of thriving trade economies and scientific achievements. An SCO space that is well-integrated has the potential to bring about new developments as well as a new era for the Eurasian region and beyond. Numerous projects, including the International North-South Transport Corridor and the Chabahar port development project, are in progress to increase connectivity.

Exploring complementarities and comparative advantages can lead the region into an era of digital economy, secure cyberspace, sustainable development and environment friendly energy security. An enabling environment must be established to develop talent in emerging technology fields like artificial intelligence (AI), industrial revolution 4.0, cyber security, space engineering and medicine. Pan-SCO initiatives with real potential must be planned and carried out. A transparent and cooperative financial mechanism needs to be devised for the SCO to undertake regional initiatives and accomplish practical cooperation and carry the benefits to the common people.

People-to-people interactions and cultural exchanges are a critical aspect of international relations. Strong civilisational ties exist throughout the entire SCO region, which is distinguished by a shared Buddhist heritage. It is possible to develop tourism and travel, especially when it comes to history, architecture and spirituality, to foster greater intercultural dialogue, particularly among the young people. When showcasing the potential for business and tourism, the media's role becomes crucial.

In order to discuss these topics and advance scholarly knowledge, the Indian Council of World Affairs, in collaboration with the Ministry of External Affairs of India, organised a two-day **'International Conference on SCO: Reconnect ~ Rejuvenate'**, the first of its kind, in March 2023. It was unique in the sense that all the members, observers and dialogue partners were invited to participate in the conference. The two-day academic engagement was not only lively and vibrant, but also extremely well-received by the invited countries.

One of the objectives of the conference was to welcome the newcomers to the SCO academic family and take in fresh viewpoints from North Africa and West Asia. It also involved assessing and comprehending the ramifications of the most recent events in and around the SCO. The organisation's initiatives and progress in different areas were evaluated critically by the participants. They also offered ideas on how to improve the SCO region's practical cooperation even further. Another important objective of the conference was to revive the dialogue among the academics in the area, in the post-pandemic context.

The event was held in hybrid format and attended by ambassadors, practitioners, experts and academicians from the SCO member, observer and dialogue partner countries. The Deputy Secretary General of the SCO, Ambassador Grigory Logvinov, attended in person on behalf of the Secretariat. Apart from the plenary and concluding sessions, the conference comprised of four working sessions: "Reconnect and Lead: SCO's Role in Enhanced Integration"; "Reconnect for Stability: Ensuring Secure Re-Emergence of Eurasia"; "Reconnect, Synchronise, Grow: Quest for Enhanced Connectivity"; and "Reconnecting the People: Invigorating Hearts & Minds". Some papers were presented in English, while the non-English papers are official/unofficial translations of the presentations made during the conference. The chapters of the book have generally been organised as per the SCO's practice of the order of precedence.

The book's opening chapter examines how political and economic scenarios are developing throughout Eurasia, from Kazakhstan's point of view. It views the conflict between Russia and Ukraine as the catalyst for a dramatic shift in Eurasia. It suggests that Moscow and Beijing will strengthen their relations in the wake of sanctions on Russia. Moscow needs this alliance more than Beijing does. At the same time, China will not sacrifice its interests for the sake of Moscow. China-US competition is seen as another source of geopolitical tension in Eurasia. The paper proposes transforming the SCO into a potent trans-regional economic platform. It calls for an increased Indian presence in Central Asia, including through investments and technological cooperation.

The viewpoint from China is presented in the second chapter. It talks about the challenges facing the SCO, including the developments in Afghanistan, the coronavirus pandemic and the Ukrainian crisis. Armed conflicts have broken out between certain countries within the region. The SCO region is now in a challenging and complicated situation as a result of these incidents. Four primary challenges are identified in the paper: the conflict between Russia and the West; unconventional security issues; strengthening regional cooperation; and how to respond to the demands of the circumstances? It calls for increased inter-regional security cooperation, sub-regional economic cooperation and active SCO participation in global governance.

The Kyrgyz scholar's paper describes the SCO as a powerful trans-regional organisation that personifies the philosophies of inclusiveness and collaboration. The SCO promotes cooperation, respect for one another and equal treatment for all its member states. According to the paper, the SCO's inclusive and collaborative philosophy provides a welcome contrast to the conventional power dynamics, which frequently place a higher priority on dominance or competition. The researcher names a number of areas where engagement can be improved, including academic research, digital connectivity, humanitarian cooperation, energy cooperation and the preservation of cultural heritage. It also emphasises how crucial youth cooperation is within the SCO region and underscores the need to protect the youth from the influence of terrorist organisations and extremist movements, which exploit their vulnerability.

The diversity of civilisational identities and legacies in the SCO area has been highlighted in the paper by a Pakistani scholar in the next chapter. It emphasises togetherness through shared ideals of peaceful coexistence. In addition, it underlines the necessity to develop new models for the empowerment of women. The chapter offers a range of policy recommendations to help revitalise the concept of peaceful coexistence, thereby enhancing the vibrancy and dynamic nature of the SCO space.

The author of the following chapter, a scholar from Tajikistan, notes that in order to create the most successful model of trade and economic cooperation within the SCO and to forge new and old partnerships, it is urgent to look for and identify non-standard approaches. It states that the difficulties may become grave threats if coordinated preventive adaptation measures are not implemented. In order to develop an open, transparent, inclusive and non-discriminatory international trading system, the paper suggests implementing cooperative projects, exchanging best practices and experience and finding ways to expand cooperation in the area of sustainable and balanced development.

An Uzbek perspective on the systemic changes in the global order is presented in the sixth chapter. It suggests that the SCO should keep up its adherence to the values of international cooperation, openness to constructive discourse and non-alignment. It emphasises that in order to achieve equitable and mutually beneficial cooperation based on considerations of shared interests, the SCO states must continue to be devoted to the consensus principle. Regarding expansion, the academician contends that even though the SCO family is becoming larger, Central Asia, which is situated in the centre of the continent of Eurasia, should continue to serve as its 'geographical core'. The article also discusses the different connectivity projects that Central Asia is currently engaged in.

The seventh chapter by an academician from Belarus presents the Belarusian perspective on the impact of the world's attention towards the region of the SCO on its political, security and economic development. It says that against the background of such a planetary shift, the SCO is becoming the 'designer' of a new, more just architecture of a polycentric world order. Additionally, the paper offers a vision to achieve peace and prosperity (SCO responses) in the context of on-going geopolitical shifts. The paper also mentions the contours of the 'road map' for increasing the stability in Eurasia and the SCO space through expert diplomacy.

In the following chapter, a Mongolian scholar discusses Mongolia's foreign policy strategy and its involvement with the SCO. Over the past two decades, the SCO has become increasingly significant and influential in the region. Since 2004, when Mongolia became the SCO's first observer state, it has been an active participant in the organisation. According to the paper, Mongolia is eager to further cooperation with the organisation, believing that there are a lot of opportunities to develop mutually beneficial cooperation with the SCO member states and observers, including in the field of economy and maintaining regional security.

An Armenian scholar discusses the nation's involvement with the organisation in the following chapter. Armenia and the SCO are strengthening their ties. The paper highlights the importance of connectivity, particularly for India, Iran, Russia and Armenia, through the International North-South Transport Corridor. It also mentions Armenia's connectivity initiatives. The difficulties with regional connectivity caused by Azerbaijan's military operations in Nagorno-Karabakh have also been discussed. The academician points out that one of Armenia's top foreign policy objectives is the thorough strengthening of its ties with India and Iran. Armenia aims to further strengthen its cooperation with the individual member states as well as the organisation as a whole, in order to promote stability in the fragile South Caucasus region.

The perspective on the SCO from Bahrain is provided in the next chapter. The presenter mentions that the SCO plays an essential role in bringing people together and building pathways for cooperation and collaboration. Culture was termed as a vital component of the SCO nations' common heritage and a source of pride for all. The paper suggests the creation of an inter-faith dialogue programme as a means of fostering mutual understanding amongst the various religions in the area. It is crucial to involve the younger generations in the preservation of the SCO heritage, especially by utilising cutting-edge and interactive techniques, such as the integration of digital technology and social media to make heritage relevant and approachable.

An Egyptian scholar provides a North African perspective on the SCO in the following chapter. The researcher proposes that the SCO's remarkable record of economic and security cooperation is the reason it has gained traction in Egypt. According to the expert, Cairo seeks the organisation's assistance to further both its national interests and its interactions with the 'Global South'. Egypt aims to widen its pool of partners. The detrimental effects of the war between Russia and Ukraine, particularly with regard to energy and food security, have served to emphasise how crucial it is to 'diversify allies' in order to bolster domestic stability. The partnership between Egypt and the SCO will support the global efforts to address issues such as the energy crises, food shortage, climate change, lack of funds for development and growing debt accumulated by the developing countries.

A Cambodian perspective on the SCO and regional developments is provided in the following chapter. It explores the important role that the SCO plays in advancing regional and global development as well as the organisation's history and evolution. A section deals with Cambodia's engagement in the SCO. It suggests that Cambodia will be able to capitalise on the economic opportunities stemming from this regional grouping. This would serve to realise the objective of Cambodia's economic diplomacy and diversification strategy. The paper suggests various ways forward for the SCO, including the role of Cambodia as a bridge to promote cooperation between ASEAN and the SCO, as it is the only country in ASEAN that holds a 'dialogue partner' status in the SCO.

Kuwait's prospects with the SCO are covered in the 12th chapter of the volume. According to the presentation, the inclusion of the Arab and Gulf nations as SCO dialogue partners highlights the platform's growing significance in the Middle East and the desire to further promote cooperation among the Asian nations. Highlighting the Afghanistan situation as a major concern, the paper says that in view of the evolving humanitarian situation in Afghanistan, Kuwait supports the continued efforts to help the Afghan people achieve their aspirations and basic needs. Cultural exchange is an additional facet of the Kuwait-SCO cooperation. Expanding cultural interactions within the SCO region, promoting mutual understanding among their peoples and respecting their cultural traditions and customs and preserving and enhancing cultural diversity within the SCO space will remain a high priority for the country.

The Maldives' relationship and future prospects with the SCO are discussed in the following chapter. The presenter appreciated the sovereign equality of all the states in the organisation. The chapter underlines the significance of sustaining peace and prompting sustainable development. For sustaining peace, understating of cultural diversity and tolerance towards each other to appreciate differences are indispensable. The academician cited the United Arab Emirates as an example of a country with an effective programme aimed at fostering a happy culture among its people. The 'SCO Day' was proposed as a way to foster interpersonal connections.

The 15th chapter gives a perspective on the SCO from the UAE. The expert emphasised the value of connectivity, stating that it is a powerful enabler. According to the paper, the UAE's strong economy has a lot of potential for the SCO area. It offers a number of competitive advantages that have been demonstrated through time, thanks to its advantageous location, top-notch smart logistics and transportation infrastructure, multimodal connectivity corridors and free trade agreements. The trade flow between the UAE and the SCO members has increased over time as a result of the UAE's multilateral cooperation strategy, which is centred on improving connectivity through a number of initiatives. The growth of the hydrogen supply chain, especially for green hydrogen, is one possible area of cooperation. It was mentioned that the SCO has enormous potential for green hydrogen, food chain security and agriculture.

The final chapter provides a perspective on the SCO from Sri Lanka. The presenter notes that Sri Lanka values connectivity with friendly countries. In the contemporary setting, this encompasses commerce, aviation, energy, maritime, digital connectivity and interpersonal interactions. Sri Lanka is striving to become one of the top maritime hubs in the world by leveraging its exceptional geographic advantage. The ultimate goal of the Sri Lankan government is to revive its historical legacy in order to build a robust and advanced green economy. As Sri Lanka develops into a significant hub for finance, logistics and business, it hopes that businesses from the SCO area will think about establishing production and processing facilities there. Additionally, it backs initiatives to deepen economic, communication and transportation links between Central and South Asia in order to help realise the shared objective of security and prosperity in the SCO region.

New Delhi **Athar Zafar**

1

A Perspective from Kazakhstan

Zhumabek Sarabekov

The paper probably contains more questions than answers, because we are at the crossroads of world history and it is difficult to predict in advance the final vectors that will determine the balance of power in the strategic perspective.

One thing is clear for sure: the entire architecture of international relations and the world economy is shifting and undergoing critical transformations. Accordingly, the Eurasian countries are facing a huge number of security challenges in a rapidly changing world. At the same time, the geopolitical shifts open up new opportunities. Eurasia is now entering a period of radical transformation and one of the main triggers is the war in Ukraine, which is essentially a proxy war between Russia and the West. We see that the conflict is dragging on and it makes the risk of a direct conflict between Russia and NATO increasingly real.

Such a situation creates one of the most dangerous moments in the history of the entire Eurasian continent. At the same time, even without nuclear escalation, it will be very difficult to put out the flames of the Ukrainian war, because even an approximate formula for a peaceful settlement remains unclear.

One of the most significant consequences of the Ukrainian crisis is the fundamental split between Russia and Europe. Even if the Ukrainian crisis de-escalates, there will not be a one-step rapprochement. A number of Western and Russian experts even claim that the "point of no return" has been passed in Russia-West relations.

As a result, Russia finds itself in a very difficult situation and has to focus and rely mostly on China. The outcome of President Xi Jinping's recent visit to Moscow shows that Moscow and Beijing will strengthen relations, even in the face of sanctions. However, we understand that Moscow needs this alliance much more than Beijing does. It is also obvious that China will not sacrifice its interests for the sake of Moscow. At the same time, it is also clear that despite the large-scale sanctions, the complete isolation of Russia is impossible, given its remaining power capabilities, as well as its solid position in global commodity markets.

The growing confrontation between China and the United States is another source of geopolitical tension in Eurasia. In particular, the Ukrainian conflict has highlighted the issue of Taiwan. Washington suspects Beijing of preparing for a military operation to reunite Taiwan with China by force and the US is increasing arms shipments to Taipei.

We should also take note of the growing confrontation between China and the US in the field of high technology, which threatens to divide the global market into opposing technological camps.

A storm is rising, not only in global politics, but also in the economic architecture of Eurasia. Today, we are witnessing a massive destruction of the economic ties that have been built over the last 30 years. The global logistics of energy supplies in Eurasia is also changing. Therefore, the war in Ukraine is forcing a breakdown of the global system and creating a new reality.

Against this background, the prospects for the SCO also look encouraging. Moreover, it is the SCO that could become the platform for the new emerging international order in Eurasia. First, of course, is the organisation's economic potential, which is enormous, but still unrealised. Now, more than half of the world's population lives in the SCO countries and about 25 percent of the gross world product (GWP) is created here – more than US$ 23 trillion.

The SCO region has a powerful intellectual and technological potential and a significant part of the world's energy resources - coal, metals and renewable energy sources. Therefore, it is necessary to transform the SCO into an effective trans-regional economic platform. The successful future of the SCO lies precisely in turning the organisation into a highly functional economic platform.

It is the stimulation of mutual trade and investment, as well as the expansion of energy and transport links that should be focused on, because in terms of geopolitics, the SCO members have different aspirations and this is unlikely to change in the foreseeable future.

More active investment ties among the SCO members would also be useful for maintaining the geopolitical balance within the organisation. For example, the Central Asian countries need alternative investment partners to China and Russia and India can be an important player here.

It needs to be emphasised here that our region objectively needs a larger Indian presence in the form of investments and technological solutions. The fact is that the economic indicators remain very modest. For example, India's trade with the Central Asian countries accounts for only 0.2-0.4 percent of India's total foreign trade. China's trade with Central Asia is almost 30 times higher than that of India and Russia's trade with Central Asia is about 20 times higher.

It is, therefore, important for India and the Central Asian countries to intensify their economic partnerships. India's presence in the region should be supported by sufficient political and financial resources. In this regard, new meetings on the format of the India-Central Asia Summit, with the participation of heads of state, heads of governments as well as the representatives of big businesses are necessary. It would be better to hold the summit, not online, but in the form of live meetings.

An additional factor that could strengthen the dynamics of the economic partnerships could be the conclusion of a free trade agreement between India and the Eurasian Economic Union (EAEU). As it is known, negotiations are already underway.

Negotiations on the International North-South Transport Corridor (INSTC), which is expected to increase the access of Indian goods to the markets of Central Asia, require a separate discussion. There is also a need for systematic work between the relevant agencies of our countries.

Secondly, the objective of the SCO and the composition of its members correspond to the spirit of multipolarity. The SCO has already developed a unique partnership formula based on mutual trust and equal and open dialogue.

It is obvious that the potential of the SCO will only grow in the future. We are talking, of course, about further expansion. The question of Turkey's accession to the group begs to be answered objectively. Ankara has probably already expressed an interest in joining the SCO.

It would be wrong, of course, to focus only on the economic track. The second priority will, undoubtedly, remain the sphere of security and the SCO could play a more active role in the stabilisation of the situation in Afghanistan. Of course, the task of combating terrorism, extremism and drug trafficking remains relevant.

In conclusion, it can be said that the SCO has already established itself as a universally recognised and powerful association and is a key factor in the security of the Eurasian continent. At the same time, new geo-economic prospects are now opening up before the SCO. It is very important for experts and the analytical community to meet in order to realise these new opportunities.

2

Situation and Tasks Facing the SCO in the Midst of Great Change

Deng Hao

Three issues may be mentioned briefly regarding the current situation facing the SCO, as well as the orientation of its future development: first, what are the main challenges and trials facing the SCO at the present time; second, what are the main opportunities for the SCO in the new situation; and third, on which areas the SCO will need to focus its efforts in the face of the new situation and challenges.

We can start with the first question. We all know that in recent years, the situation in the SCO region has not been calm. The changes in Afghanistan, the coronavirus pandemic and the Ukrainian crisis followed one after the other. Within the region, 'hot spots' are also frequently observed: internal unrest occurs in some countries and large-scale armed border conflicts break out between some countries. These incidents have led to a complex and difficult situation in the SCO region, not seen since its inception.

In general, the SCO is currently facing challenges and trials in four aspects. First, the relations between Russia, the US and the West have moved from a struggle to a complete break and full-scale confrontation and geopolitical factors have become the most serious test and challenge for the SCO. How to treat the American and Western factors became an urgent issue for the SCO. Based on a full consideration of the complexity and diversity of the relationship between the member states, the US and the West, how could the 'original intention' of the SCO to promote the establishment of a new, fair and reasonable international political and economic order be adhered to? How could the SCO insist on maintaining international justice and at the same time, not fall into the trap of a new cold war with the US and the West and prevent a new confrontation between the camps? All this will, undoubtedly, become a serious test for the SCO.

Secondly, as the security situation becomes more complex and volatile, the security issue clearly becomes more important than that of development, one that the SCO must address as a matter of priority. How to effectively prevent the confrontations between the major powers from escalating? How to effectively help the countries to secure their rights? How to mediate in and mitigate border conflicts between the concerned countries and how to better respond to various emerging non-traditional security challenges? These are also urgent problems facing the SCO.

Thirdly, with the intensification of the global and regional economic downturn, the problems of the development of the SCO are becoming increasingly more complex and serious. How to carry out regional cooperation more effectively to help the member countries overcome their difficulties and prevent the collapse of the regional development of the economy is undoubtedly an urgent issue in SCO cooperation.

Fourthly, since the SCO has rarely spoken out or acted in a number of regional crises, the problem of the lack of action and effectiveness of the SCO has, once again, come to the fore. How to respond to the needs of the situation, confront the problems of the lack of action and effectiveness of the SCO and find ways to solve them? How to introduce innovative decision-making methods and increase the effectiveness of cooperation based on the principle of consensus and 'constructive intervention' in regional emergencies and conflicts between countries? Obviously, all these questions are a real problem for the SCO, which can no longer be avoided or postponed indefinitely.

Now, the next question is about the possibilities for the development of the SCO in the new situation. The word 'crisis' in Chinese consists of two parts: 'danger' and 'opportunity' and means that 'in danger, there are opportunities'. So, what are the opportunities for the SCO in the current situation? It can be said that the biggest opportunity for the SCO lies in the fact that the advanced concept and soft power of the SCO is becoming more and more attractive, not only to its member states, but also to other countries. As the existing international order becomes more fragmented and the existing mechanisms of global governance more and more dysfunctional, the SCO has already become the preferred choice for multilateral relations among the regional countries. This is evidenced by the increase in the number of countries applying for the membership of the SCO.

Since eight Eurasian countries have joined the SCO, the overall strength and international influence of the SCO has been further strengthened and the scope of regional cooperation has been greatly expanded. The latter forms a much larger market and space for energy cooperation and interconnection and also creates favourable conditions for the SCO to play a more important role in global and regional governance. It can be said that the SCO has become the main source of hope for maintaining regional stability and promoting regional prosperity. There is great potential and a wide perspective for future development.

Finally, the priorities and main tasks of the SCO in the future may be discussed briefly. First, in response to the intensification of the game of powers, the SCO should participate more actively in global governance. By adhering to the values and norms of the 'Shanghai Spirit' based on the principles of "non-alignment, non-confrontation and non-anti-third party", using consensus as a decision-making tool and establishing the ultimate goal of building a community of common destiny, the SCO should strive to find, for all the countries of the world and especially for the SCO countries, such a path that will overcome the Cold War mentality. Thus, the SCO will fairly and actively defend international fairness and justice.

Second, in response to increased security threats, the SCO should take more active steps in security cooperation. On the one hand, it should endow the Regional Anti-Terrorist Structure (RATS) of the SCO in Tashkent with broad functions, powers and capabilities, so that it really becomes the main pillar and operational mechanism of the SCO in the fight against threats and challenges to regional security. On the other hand, it should develop closer cooperation with organisations such as the Collective Security Treaty Organisation (CSTO) and the Conference on Interaction and Confidence-Building Measures in Asia (CICA) and also strive to form joint efforts to maintain regional security and stability.

Third, in response to more serious developmental problems, the SCO should vigorously advocate for sub-regional and small-scale multilateral cooperation and actively seek new ways out of the structural dilemma of economic cooperation through new forms, such as the creation of model demonstration zones and bases. At the same time, institutional cooperation should be a priority and the focus of SCO economic cooperation. The SCO should strive to create a favourable environment for the development of member states.

It is also necessary to actively change the existing approach of cooperation, in order to ensure its sustainable development, gradually moving from government-led cooperation towards the direction of both government-led and market-based functioning.

Fourth, in order to address the shortcomings of the SCO's operational capacity, it should acknowledge its own shortcomings, steadily promote internal reforms, effectively address and balance fairness and efficiency as well as power and commitment, constantly improve the effectiveness of cooperation and strive to ensure that the SCO truly transforms itself from a conference mechanism into cooperation.

3

Strengthening Cooperation and Empowering Youth: Key Themes at the SCO Conference

Altynai Kanatbekovna Aliiaskarova

Abstract
The recently concluded International Conference, titled "Reconnect ~ Rejuvenate", organised by the Indian Council of World Affairs (ICWA) in New Delhi, provided a unique platform for experts to exchange views, share experiences and foster meaningful dialogue. The conference, hosted by the Shanghai Cooperation Organisation (SCO) Study Centre of ICWA, highlighted the organisation's commitment to human rights, equal treatment and the protection of humanity. The SCO is an influential trans-regional organisation that embodies the philosophy of inclusion and collaboration. The SCO advocates for equal treatment, mutual respect and cooperation among all the member states. It goes beyond tolerance and embraces a spirit of genuine dialogue and shared prosperity, recognising that strength lies in unity and the exchange of diverse perspectives. The SCO's progress is evident in its achievements of strengthening trust, promoting security, countering common challenges and aligning with initiatives like China's 'One Belt – One Road'. Additionally, the SCO emphasises humanitarian cooperation, digital connectivity, academic collaboration, energy cooperation and the preservation of cultural heritage. Empowering youth, preserving cultural heritage and promoting education

and collaboration are strategic imperatives that enhance the SCO's vision of an interconnected, harmonious and inclusive world.

Key words: SCO, regional progress, immersion in cultural heritage, youth empowerment.

SCO's Philosophy of Inclusion and Collaboration

To set the tone, a quote from Mohandas Karamchand Gandhi, known as the Father of the Indian Nation, may be cited: "I do not want my house to be walled-in on all sides and my windows to be stuffed. I want the cultures of all the lands to be blown about my house as freely as possible. But I refuse to be blown off my feet by any. I refuse to live in other people's houses as an interloper, a beggar or a slave."[1] This sentiment embodies the spirit of the SCO, which advocates equal treatment and mutual respect among all nations, regardless of their size, wealth or strength.

In addition to the inspiring quote by Mahatma Gandhi, the philosophy of inclusion and collaboration embraced by the SCO holds profound implications for fostering a more interconnected and harmonious world. By promoting the values of inclusivity, the SCO recognises the importance of acknowledging diverse perspectives, cultures and histories and encourages mutual understanding among its member states.

One of the most intriguing aspects of the SCO's philosophy is its emphasis on bridging gaps and building bridges across geographical, cultural and ideological divides. This approach goes beyond mere tolerance or coexistence and instead, seeks to cultivate an environment of genuine cooperation, dialogue and shared prosperity. It recognises that true strength lies, not in isolation, but in unity, where nations can draw upon each other's strengths and learn from their unique experiences.

Furthermore, the SCO's philosophy of inclusion and collaboration offers a refreshing alternative to traditional power dynamics, which often prioritise dominance or competition. By embracing the idea that all nations, regardless of their size or wealth, have valuable contributions to offer, the SCO encourages the empowerment of smaller nations and allows for a more equitable distribution of influence. This approach promotes a more balanced and multipolar world order, where every member state has a voice and an opportunity to shape the global agenda.

Another interesting aspect of the SCO's philosophy is its recognition that collaboration extends beyond the realm of politics and economics. It acknowledges the interconnectedness of various sectors, including culture, education, science and technology. By fostering cooperation in these domains, the SCO creates avenues for the exchange of ideas, innovations and knowledge, leading to mutual growth and development.

Moreover, the SCO's philosophy of inclusion and collaboration extends beyond its member states. Through dialogue and partnerships with observer states, dialogue partners and international organisations, the SCO seeks to build bridges beyond its immediate sphere of influence. This approach not only strengthens regional stability, but also contributes to global peace, security and sustainable development.

In summary, the SCO's philosophy of inclusion and collaboration, as epitomised by Mahatma Gandhi's quote, serves as a powerful reminder of the importance of embracing diversity, respecting the autonomy of nations and striving for cooperation, rather than competition. By fostering an environment of mutual respect, understanding and shared prosperity, the SCO paves the way for a more interconnected, harmonious and inclusive world, where the cultures of all nations can freely coexist and thrive.

SCO's Progress and Objectives

The SCO's remarkable growth as a dynamically evolving trans-regional organisation has been acknowledged. With nearly half of the world's population and 25 percent of the global GDP among its member states, the SCO has successfully achieved its goals of strengthening mutual trust, promoting security and stability and countering common challenges and threats. Moreover, the significance of aligning the SCO's objectives with China's 'One Belt – One Road' initiative, a transformative international infrastructure project that fosters economic partnerships, improves infrastructure and enhances cultural interaction among participating nations, can be highlighted.

Building upon the previous points, here are some additional interesting aspects to consider regarding the SCO's progress and objectives:

- **Humanitarian Cooperation:** The SCO places great importance on humanitarian cooperation as part of its broader objectives. It engages in joint efforts to address natural disasters, public health emergencies and humanitarian crises within the region. Through coordinated disaster response mechanisms and sharing of best practices, the SCO member states work together to provide timely assistance and support to affected communities, thus demonstrating solidarity and compassion.
- **Digital Connectivity:** Recognising the increasing significance of digital technologies in shaping the global landscape, the SCO has prioritised digital connectivity as a means to promote economic growth and

development. It seeks to bridge the digital divide within its member states and enhance cooperation in areas such as e-commerce, digital infrastructure and cybersecurity. By fostering a digitally connected region, the SCO aims to unleash the potential of emerging technologies and promote inclusive digital development.

- **Academic and Research Collaboration:** The SCO emphasises academic and research collaboration among its member states, thereby facilitating the exchange of knowledge, expertise and innovations. It promotes joint research projects, academic exchanges and scholarships to enhance educational cooperation. This emphasis on intellectual cooperation contributes to the development of a knowledge-based society, fostering innovation and cultivating future leaders within the SCO region.
- **Energy Cooperation:** The SCO recognises the importance of energy security and cooperation in sustaining economic growth and development. It facilitates collaboration among member states in areas such as energy exploration, production and transit as well as promoting the use of renewable and clean energy sources. By enhancing energy cooperation, the SCO aims to ensure a stable and sustainable energy supply for its member states, thus contributing to their overall development and resilience.
- **Cultural Heritage Preservation:** The SCO places significance on preserving and promoting the rich cultural heritage of its member states. Recognising the value of cultural diversity and its role in fostering mutual understanding and respect, the SCO supports initiatives that safeguard historical sites, artefacts and intangible cultural heritage. By preserving cultural heritage, the SCO contributes to the promotion of cultural tourism, intercultural dialogue and the preservation of shared historical legacies.

In summary, the SCO's progress extends beyond traditional security and economic cooperation. Its focus on humanitarian cooperation, digital connectivity, academic collaboration, energy cooperation and cultural heritage preservation reflects its commitment to the holistic development of its member states and addressing their evolving needs. By embracing these diverse areas of collaboration, the SCO continues to evolve as a comprehensive platform for regional integration, stability and sustainable development.

Empowering Youth: A Strategic Imperative and Strengthening the 'Shanghai Spirit' Through Youth Exchanges

The SCO region has a population of over 3.2 billion people and the youth account for more than 55 percent of it. This underscores the imperative of creating an enabling environment for the younger generation to thrive. The youth within each SCO member state embody the potential for innovation and progress, making their empowerment a strategic advantage for the entire region.

The Joint Appeal and Action Plan adopted during the SCO Qingdao Summit held in 2018, reaffirms the significance of education, moral guidance and cultivating a thirst for knowledge among young people. There is a critical need to protect the youth from the influence of terrorist organisations and extremist movements, which exploit their vulnerability. The SCO member states have called upon the international community to join forces in countering the involvement of the youth in such destructive activities.

It is important to strengthen the conditions for youth cooperation and mutual understanding as well as the role of the SCO Youth Council. This council, which convenes annually, provides a platform for promoting youth entrepreneurship and implementing special programmes to enhance the business acumen of young entrepreneurs across the SCO region.

It is also significant to foster stronger bonds and promote the 'Shanghai Spirit' through intensified youth exchanges. Deeply immersing young people in this spirit, which embodies mutual trust, good neighbourliness and the integration of diverse civilisations, allows the SCO member states to forge stronger connections and pursue common objectives. By enhancing youth exchanges, the SCO aims to cultivate mutual trust and good neighbourliness among the member states, facilitate effective cooperation in various fields such as politics, trade, economy, science, technology and culture, ensure peace, security and stability in the region and contribute to the establishment of a democratic, fair and rational international order.

Empowering the youth within the SCO region is not only a strategic necessity, but also a means to nurture the 'Shanghai Spirit' and foster a shared sense of purpose among future leaders. By investing in their education, providing them with opportunities for skill development and encouraging cross-cultural exchanges, the SCO member states lay a solid foundation for a prosperous and harmonious future, built upon the principles of trust, cooperation and respect.

Preserving and Promoting Cultural Heritage

The rich cultural heritage of the SCO countries, characterised by the contributions of eminent thinkers, scientists and explorers throughout history has been acknowledged. The SCO member states share numerous historical and cultural connections, common traditions, languages, ethnic and cultural similarities and good-neighbourly relations. Preserving and promoting this cultural heritage is not only a source of pride, but also an essential element in fostering mutual understanding and strengthening bonds among the younger generation.

To ensure the preservation of cultural heritage, the SCO recognises the importance of adopting a multifaceted approach. This involves developing educational programmes that integrate the study of cultural heritage with curricula, thus teaching the youth about the history, art, music, literature and architecture of their respective countries. By fostering a sense of appreciation for their cultural roots, the SCO member states can instill a sense of identity and belonging among the youth.

In addition, organising cultural events that showcase the diverse traditions and customs within the SCO region can provide platforms for cross-cultural exchange and dialogue. Festivals, exhibitions and cultural exchanges provide firsthand experiences of the richness and diversity of SCO nations to the young people, thus deepening their understanding of the same and forging meaningful connections.

The SCO also recognises the potential of digital technologies in preserving and promoting cultural heritage. By leveraging digital platforms and resources, the organisation can create virtual museums, digital archives and interactive educational materials, making cultural heritage more accessible and engaging for the younger generation. This approach not only ensures the preservation of artefacts and historical records, but also harnesses technology to transmit knowledge and ignite curiosity among the youth.

Another important aspect of preserving and promoting cultural heritage is the collaboration with youth organisations and the media. Engaging young people in cultural preservation initiatives, such as heritage conservation projects or community-based cultural programs, fosters a sense of ownership and pride in their heritage.

Furthermore, partnering with media outlets to showcase the diverse cultural expressions and talents of SCO member states can help raise awareness and appreciation among a wider audience, both within and outside the region. By actively preserving and promoting cultural heritage, the SCO member states not only preserve their unique identities, but also contribute to the sustainable development of the region.

Cultural heritage acts as a bridge between generations, providing a shared sense of history and collective memory. It fosters an environment where young people can explore their roots, celebrate diversity and build a future that is grounded in mutual understanding and respect. The SCO's commitment to preserving and promoting cultural heritage is crucial for nurturing a sense of identity, fostering mutual understanding and building lasting connections among the younger generation. By integrating cultural heritage education, organising cultural events, harnessing digital technologies and collaborating with youth organisations and the media, the SCO member states can ensure that their rich cultural legacies continue to thrive and inspire generations to come.

Recognising the significance of traditional craftsmanship in preserving cultural heritage, the SCO member states place great emphasis on supporting and revitalising traditional artisanal practices. These age-old crafts, passed down through generations, embody the skills, techniques and artistic expressions of the SCO's diverse cultures.

By nurturing and promoting traditional craftsmanship, the SCO member states can not only safeguard their unique cultural identities, but also contribute to the economic empowerment of local communities. Artisans and craftsmen play a vital role in preserving traditional techniques, whether in pottery, weaving, woodcarving, metalwork or intricate embroidery. Their expertise and creativity infuse contemporary designs with a touch of heritage, creating products that are both culturally authentic and commercially appealing.

The SCO encourages initiatives that provide training and capacity-building opportunities for artisans, thereby ensuring the continuity of traditional craftsmanship. Collaborative projects among member states promote the exchange of knowledge and skills, enabling artisans to learn from each other and enrich their crafts. These initiatives also seek to empower artisans by facilitating access to markets, both within the region and globally, thus allowing their unique creations to be appreciated and valued by a wider audience.

Recognising the potential of digital platforms, the SCO supports the documentation and promotion of traditional craftsmanship through online platforms and e-commerce. By creating dedicated websites and digital marketplaces, artisans gain exposure to a global audience, thereby showcasing their exceptional skills and cultural heritage to enthusiasts around the world. Such digital initiatives not only provide economic opportunities, but also serve as a means to create awareness about the importance of preserving traditional craftsmanship and the cultural heritage it represents.

Through their commitment to support traditional craftsmanship, the SCO member states honour the invaluable contributions of artisans and craftsmen who safeguard their cultural heritage. By valuing and promoting these artisanal traditions, the SCO not only ensures the preservation of tangible and intangible cultural assets, but also celebrates the living legacy of their rich and diverse cultures.

Education and Collaboration for Youth Development: Nurturing Future Innovators and Global Citizens

Beyond its fundamental role in supporting the youth, education stands as a powerful catalyst for transformation, unlocking the full potential of young minds. Apart from cooperation on education, there is a need for innovative and collaborative approaches to empower the youth in the SCO region.

In a world driven by rapid advancements, the importance of harnessing emerging technologies and interdisciplinary knowledge in preparing the young people for the challenges and opportunities of the future needs to be recognised. Building upon this vision, the SCO member states pledged to fully tap into the potential of the SCO University, envisaging it as a dynamic hub for joint training and research initiatives. By leveraging the diverse expertise and resources of member states, the SCO University can offer specialised programmes in high-demand areas and cutting-edge fields, ranging from renewable energy and sustainable ecology to nanotechnology, IT and regional studies. These joint training opportunities will not only equip young individuals with advanced technical skills, but also foster collaboration, innovation and a cross-pollination of ideas among the youth of the region.

There is a need to expand scholarship opportunities and include more educational institutions from the SCO member states within the SCO University framework. This inclusive approach will ensure that talented and deserving young individuals from diverse backgrounds are provided with access to quality education. By creating additional scholarships, especially for the underprivileged and marginalised youth, the SCO members can actively work towards reducing educational disparities and promoting social inclusion. Simultaneously, the inclusion of a broader range of educational institutions from the member states enriches the educational landscape, providing a wealth of perspectives and fostering an environment of vibrant academic exchange.

While equipping the youth with knowledge and skills is crucial, the significance of holistic development and the cultivation of the concept of global citizenship are also important. The SCO member states acknowledged the importance of fostering values such as cultural understanding, empathy and social responsibility among the youth. To this end, they pledged to promote intercultural dialogue, language learning and exchange programmes that encourage young people to explore and appreciate the diversity within the SCO region. By nurturing a sense of global citizenship, the SCO member states can empower the youth to become active contributors to their countries and the region, thereby fostering a harmonious and interconnected world.

Educational cooperation within the SCO region serves as a cornerstone for youth development, unlocking opportunities for personal growth, economic prosperity and social cohesion. By prioritising collaboration, innovative approaches and the holistic development of young minds, the SCO member states can cultivate a generation of forward-thinking leaders who are equipped with the necessary skills, knowledge and values to drive progress. Through education, the youth of the SCO region will shape a future that not only benefits their own countries, but also contributes to a more prosperous, inclusive and sustainable world.

Conclusion

In conclusion, the SCO embodies a philosophy of inclusion, collaboration and mutual respect among nations, as epitomised by the inspiring words of Mahatma Gandhi. The SCO's commitment to embracing diversity, promoting unity and fostering cooperation goes beyond traditional power dynamics and sets the stage for a more interconnected, harmonious and inclusive world.

The SCO's progress and objectives reflect its comprehensive approach to regional integration, stability and sustainable development. From humanitarian cooperation and digital connectivity to academic collaboration, energy cooperation and the preservation of cultural heritage, the SCO recognises the importance of addressing diverse areas of collaboration to meet the evolving needs of its member states.

Empowering the youth is a strategic imperative for the SCO, given the former's significant presence in the region. By creating an enabling environment for young people to thrive, promoting education and strengthening the 'Shanghai Spirit' through youth exchanges, the SCO cultivates a shared sense of purpose and nurtures the next generation of leaders who embody the principles of trust, cooperation and respect.

Preserving and promoting cultural heritage within the SCO region is essential for fostering mutual understanding and strengthening bonds among the youth. By adopting a multifaceted approach that includes education, cultural events, digital technologies and collaboration with youth organisations and the media, the SCO member states ensure that their rich cultural legacies continue to thrive, bridging the past with the present and inspiring future generations.

Education and collaboration are crucial for youth development, equipping young individuals with the knowledge, skills and values needed for the challenges of the future. The SCO's commitment to harnessing emerging technologies, interdisciplinary knowledge and global citizenship cultivates a generation of innovative and socially responsible leaders who will contribute to the progress and well-being of their countries and the world at large.

The SCO's philosophy of inclusion and collaboration, its comprehensive progress and objectives, focus on empowering the youth and preserving cultural heritage and dedication to education and collaboration for youth development contribute to the organisation's vision of a prosperous, interconnected and harmonious future. By embracing these principles and working together, the SCO paves the way for a more inclusive, sustainable and mutually beneficial world for generations to come.

Note

1. "Quotes of Gandhi" in original English with both the Kyrgyz and the Russian translations, p. 65.

   The Centre of Gandhian Studies at the Bishkek Humanities University, Bishkek, with the assistance of the Embassy of India, Bishkek, has decided to bring out this collection of "Quotes of Gandhi" in original English, with both the Kyrgyz and the Russian translations.

4

Reconnecting Hearts and Rejuvenating Minds in SCO Spaces: Featuring Assets of Pakistan

Ume Farwa

Abstract

Chaos, disorder, the transition of global power and the global environment are the most recurring themes of the contemporary era, urging joint efforts for ensuring the peace and prosperity of the common masses. In this milieu, the Shanghai Cooperation Organisation (SCO) is an emerging organisation that aspires to cooperate and collaborate among its member states for the resolution of common issues and threats in the region, which is rich in the diversity of civilisational identities and legacies. Therefore, in this context, this paper highlights why there is a need to implement new and innovative models of bringing people closer through the common threads of the philosophy of peaceful coexistence, enhancing the role of cultural and civilisational diplomacy by celebrating the diversity of the SCO region. Regarding this subject, the paper features assets of Pakistan including its centuries-old spiritual legacy and wisdom – Sufism and Sufi culture – architecture, music, arts, literature and festivals that establish Islamabad in the SCO spaces as a binding force in the region. It also briefly highlights the urgency to draw up new models for empowering women and concludes with a range of policy recommendations from theoretical to practical domains in making the SCO spaces more vibrant and dynamic in promoting the much-needed idea of carving a shared destiny together by reinvigorating the spirit of peaceful coexistence in its true letter and spirit. Particularly, it offers a new model of 'Celebrating Unity in Diversity' based on the thoughts and practices of Pakistan's Sufi scholar, Khawaja Shamsuddin Azeemi.

Key Words: Sufism, Sufis of Pakistan, Buddhism, SCO, Civilisational Diplomacy.

Introduction

> "Don't be satisfied with stories, how things have gone with others. Unfold your own myth."
>
> ...Rumi

From its outset, the SCO established its foundations on the principles of the 'Shanghai Spirit', urging for "mutual trust, mutual benefit, equal rights, consultations, respect for the diversity of cultures and aspiration towards common development." Its main objective was "to promote good, friendly, relations in the neighbourhood and strengthen mutual confidence among the member countries, while encouraging cooperation in all areas of interaction including defence, political, economic, socio-cultural and environmental issues, health care and others." The SCO Secretary General has reiterated the organisation's vision saying, "The SCO has an extensive agenda and it is extremely positive, aimed at creative international interaction."

Since the SCO region has its civilisational legacies and identities – the Chinese, Russian, Buddhist, Hindu and Islamic civilisations are the few prominent ones – the need to pay attention to this factor assumes great significance. If not given the right direction, the civilisational identities and legacies can erupt into large-scale conflicts. From this perspective, therefore, there is a need to employ the timeless heritage of spirituality – which is a shared legacy of all the SCO members – to open new pathways for the SCO family members to feature their assets for consolidating the movement of goodwill and lasting peace.

In this regard, Pakistan, as an active member of the SCO and being rich in spiritual heritage and wisdom, has a great deal to offer at the platform of the SCO. It has always supported the SCO family in providing further momentum to their efforts of bringing development and progress, promoting cooperation and providing an impetus to the joint drive for peaceful coexistence. Therefore, this paper has been written in this context with the intent to feature Pakistan's assets for reconnecting hearts and rejuvenating minds in the SCO spaces.

First, this paper discusses why there is a need to 'Reconnect' and 'Rejuvenate' hearts and minds in the SCO spaces. Then, it briefly dwells upon the inevitable role that spirituality would play in this aspect and features the assets of Pakistan for the promotion of human interactions and nurturing foreign relations among the SCO family. At the end, this paper presents policy recommendations for drawing a future course of interactions that are oriented towards celebrating diversity, instead of clashing due to diversity.

Why 'Reconnect' and 'Rejuvenate' SCO Spaces?

In recent times, when the old global norms are declining and new ones are rising, there cannot be any better subject to discuss among the SCO community than to chart the way forward along the lines of 'reconnecting' hearts and 'rejuvenating minds'. However, two questions must be addressed: Firstly, what is the 'disconnect' that the SCO family is trying to 'reconnect'? Secondly, what is the legacy and shared heritage that it has identified to 'rejuvenate'?

On the issue of 'reconnect', it is important to know what 'disconnect' is. Though it sounds like a cliché, yet, the fact remains that the world is in the throes of a huge transformation, which is causing a 'disconnect' from the world that was rebuilt in the post-WWII era. The biggest 'disconnect' manifested in the form of 'disorder of the neo-liberal global order.' However, that is an altogether different debate about whether it was a sustainable order to begin with. While the international system has been going through a transition phase, many changes come to light. The rise of the 'Global South' and the decline of the 'Global North' is a case in point. This shift of power leads to the questioning of the global norms that were mostly created by the Western powers. With the rise of the Asian powers, not only the norms, but also the institutions that were built on them became inadequate to cater to the needs of the rising powers.

However, following the rise of the Asian powers, these myopic constructs no longer seem in vogue in international relations. After the decline of the Western powers, a sporadic rise of the rest is prominent and is gaining momentum now. With this, not only the previously followed global norms, but also the institutions fell short of catering to the needs of the rising powers.

Therefore, in this context, it will not be unfair to maintain that the Global South needs to reconnect. It is the need of the hour. It is especially important in recent times for three reasons. Firstly, global power is shifting from the west to the east and much needs to be reconnected. Secondly, the global norms are changing. The neo-liberal order, which was architected by the West after World War II, is no longer fulfilling the needs of the contemporary era. Thirdly, the world is facing an unprecedented natural calamity in the form of the climate crisis, which, according to scientists, happens once every 10,000 years. The United Nations Development Programme, in its Human Development Reports, noted the alarming trends in the global ecosystem and called for unprecedented efforts as the planet Earth enters into another geological era, the Anthropocene Epoch.

When coupled with the hazardous implications of the recent COVID-19 pandemic, the need to 'reconnect' supersedes everything else. In such times, (when political issues and state affairs are working on the forefront to address these issues;?) the 'low politics', especially strengthening human linkages, must be explored.

Even at this point in time, we observe that the world has become deeply integrated and has multiple interactions. We have termed this state of interactions as a 'globalised world'. While a state is one interface of this world, there is a need for the states - especially the SCO members – to 'reconnect' what is broken and 'rejuvenate' what the SCO region, being rich in civilisational legacies, share with each other.

Introducing Sufism in the SCO Spaces

Since we are on the subject to 'reconnect' through culture, architecture, literature, great personalities, spirituality, media and tourism, the appealing and interesting concept of spirituality and how it helps us – as the SCO family members and its new entrants – to deepen linkages by other mediums, can be mentioned.

What do we Mean by Spirituality and why are we Discussing it in International Relations at the SCO Forum?

Spirituality can be better understood in the form of a global phenomenon, most commonly known as 'Sufism'. Sufis have been ambassadors of peace; their message of universal goodwill transcends boundaries. They do not belong to any one religion. They are found everywhere. The Eurasian region is rich in Sufi heritage. Iran and Central Asia are known as the cradle of Sufism. The iconic Sufi figure, Rumi, is part of the common lexicon of the international audience. South Asia, too, is replete with Sufi lore and the impact of Sufi legends is unmatchable.

In foreign relations, too, there is an ever greater need for tapping into Sufi insights to create a new and innovative model. The most prominent effort has been the initiative of the UNESCO Chair, Amitav Acharya. The British political scientist's initiative of Global IR has led to the book, *Sufism: A theoretical intervention in Global International Relations* by Deepshikha Shahi.

It is time that the SCO members discuss and chart the way forward as to how they want to create a new model of interactions among themselves, which is based on spirituality or in other words, Sufism. Here, we need to combine Sufi ethos with academic thinking and policy currents to tap into Sufi wisdom to 'reconnect' and 'rejuvenate'. So, the SCO family needs to pay attention to this aspect as the SCO region is rich in civilisational heritage. Therefore, we need to draw such an inter-civilisational model – based on Sufism – that can help them 'reconnect' and 'rejuvenate' their civilisational legacies, instead of becoming involved in clashes.

Featuring Assets of Pakistan

In this regard, Pakistan, which is rich in spiritual heritage and wisdom, has a great deal to offer at the platform of the SCO. Being an active member of the SCO, it has always supported the SCO family in order to provide further momentum to their efforts of bringing about development and progress, promoting cooperation and providing an impetus to the joint drive for peaceful coexistence. Therefore, this paper has been written in this context with the intent to feature Pakistan's assets for reconnecting hearts and rejuvenating minds in the SCO spaces.

Sufi Wisdom of Pakistan

Sufism is the mystical path of Islam – the inner path of self-knowing, inner wisdom, an esoteric knowledge. The Sufis preached love, faith, devotion and ecstasy in oneness. They embraced people from all walks of life and religions – even those who have no religious affiliations at all – with open arms and created a living culture of peace and brotherhood. Their thoughts and practices are a guiding model for creating a community of shared human heritage and celebrating unity in diversity.

Pakistan has much to offer in this context as there is no other country which has been as much influenced by Sufism as it. For Islamabad, it is not just Sufism, but a whole range of Sufi culture that has seeped into the social fabric deeply and it is due to this very reason that a famous French scholar of Sufism prefers to ascribe the Sufi ethos of South Asia – Pakistan, in particular – to the 'Sufi culture' of Pakistan. Therefore, it is not surprising that one finds Sufism to be an inalienable part of Pakistani society – be it in traditions, history, arts, literature, music or festivals. The Sufis of Pakistan have been a centre of attention for the western and eastern scholars. The former include Lal Shehbaz Qalandar, Shah Abdul Latif Bhittai, Bulhey Shah, Baba Fareed, Shah Hussain, Mian Muhammad Bakhsh and Sultan Bahu. Not only the Sufis, but Sufi culture also culminated into the initiation of organised Sufi orders known as *tariqas* or *silsila*. Pakistan has a number of Sufi orders that function in its society and have a worldwide appeal: Chishti, Naqshbandi, Soharwardi, Mevlevi, Azeemia, Qadria etc. With such a rich and profuse Sufi imprint, Pakistan stands in a position where it can offer a Sufi model of interactions among nations on the platform of the SCO.

It is for Sufi poetry that Pakistan's global music sensation, the late Nusrat Fateh Ali Khan, was hailed as 'Singing Buddha in Japan', 'Pavarotti of the East' in Paris and 'The Spirit of Islam' in London. The famous Sufi music, *sama* or *qawwali,* is recognised as divine music and has gone beyond South Asia. Pakistan's Sufi music is known for its global appeal. The 18th century Sufi poet, Bulhey Shah and his poetry is so popular that it can be heard across borders. One of his famous poems, "Bulleh, to me, I am unknown!" is famous for its musical rendition. The traditions, history, biographies, literature and arts of the Sufis and Sufism are dynamic links that can readily 'reconnect' the already existing roots of Sufism in Central Asia, Daoism in China, Hindu spirituality in India and Christian mysticism in Russia. However, the Sufi ethos is not only for religious affiliates. The eclectic spirit of Sufism goes beyond religion.

A living Sufi legend and spiritual scholar of Pakistan, Khawaja Shamsuddin Azeemi, who is also the current head of the Sufi order in Azeemia, is a shining example in this regard. The British Institute for Body, Mind and Spirituality listed him among the 100 most influential people in 2015. Mr. Azeemi is heading a Sufi order in Pakistan, which is working across the world through its meditation halls. In China, Russia, Central Asia and many other western countries, these meditation halls are working to 'reconnect' with the people across religions and ethnicities and 'rejuvenate' the ties that bind nations. This Pakistani Sufi order holds Adam Day worldwide to mark the day for celebrating 'Unity in Diversity', so that the unbreakable linkages that human beings share with each other can be rekindled.

Inter-Civilisational Model of 'Celebrating Unity in Diversity

Adam Day is a one of its kind event that Khawaja Shamsuddin Azeemi initiated in 2003, in Manchester, UK, for the celebration of 'Unity in Diversity' that exists in humankind. Since then, he hosts this event in meditation halls in Europe and America on August 10 every year. It is attended by Hindus, Muslims, Christians, Sikhs, Buddhists, Baha'is, pagans, Jews, Quakers and Brahma Kumaris. The same can be adopted in the SCO spaces for embracing its rich diversity. The main postulates, based on Adam Day, which could lay the foundation of the SCO inter-faith model of human interactions, are as follows:

- Mankind originated from a common source: the first prototype of the male human being (Adam) and female human being (Eve).
- Through this kinship, all human beings – irrespective of their religious affiliations – are brothers and sisters to one another.
- This human brotherhood does not change, no matter what the geographical location of human beings is. A human being tends to be fair-skinned when he/she lives in cold regions such as Europe, America or Russia; if he/she lives in hot regions, the human physiology makes him/her dark-skinned. The colour of the skin is a by-product of the variations in temperature.
- Ethnicities are superficial differences that exist for the mere identification of human beings.
- All religions share common absolute truths. The Prophets only taught high values of morality to their followers and advised them to practice the constructive pattern of thinking and shun the destructive one. They also taught their followers to respect the teachings of other Prophets and pay utmost regard to their followers.

Civilisational Heritage of Pakistan

From time immemorial, the land where Pakistan is situated today has been the bedrock of the world's leading civilisations. There is plenty of evidence to suggest that this land – today's Pakistan – has played host to great civilisations, even in the prehistoric times. The fossil jaws of apes *circa*/ca. 14 million years old have been discovered in Pakistan's Potohar region and the earliest human hand axe, dated around two million years ago, has also been found, which is now on display in the Islamabad museum.

Over the centuries, the land of Pakistan inherited a rich cultural and civilisational heritage that manifested itself, in different frames of time, as the Indus civilisation, Gandhara civilisation, Islamic civilisation, Sikh heritage, memoirs and relics of the British colonial period and of modern times as well.

However, in the context of SCO spaces, Pakistan's Buddhist heritage warrants a special mention. Pakistan is blessed with a rich Buddhist heritage. Pakistan is the cradle of the Gandhara civilisation, which witnessed the rise of many great empires over the centuries. These include the Persian Macedonian, Mauryan, Bactrian, Scythian of Eastern Europe, Parthian, Kushans, White Huns of Central Asia and Hindu Shahi of Northern India. Pakistan has many archaeological sites – designated as historical sites by UNESCO – including the Buddhist ruins of Takht Bai and those in the neighbouring city of Sahr-i-Bahlol. In terms of the UN historical sites of Buddhism, Pakistan has a number of them spread across the country.

Lahore: The City of Splendour in Mughal Architecture

The architecture of Pakistan is a reflection of its civilisation and Pakistan has many buildings that are its landmarks, such as the Mohatta Palace and Badshahi Mosque. Lahore, a famous city of Pakistan, is known for its cultural and archaeological sites. Lahore was the capital of the Mughal empire and transformed into an exotic hub of cross-cultural activities, traditions and norms. The modern Lahore exudes the aura of the historical splendour of the medieval times. It has also been a hub of spiritual, mystical and Sufi activities and movements in South Asia.

Charting New Pathways for Women Empowerment

Not only in the SCO region, but also in the world, women are facing the serious issues of gender inequality and gender disparity. There is an overwhelming gender imbalance, particularly with regard to the empowerment of women. As women comprise almost half of the world population, their role in the development, progress and prosperity of mankind can hardly be denied.

Unfortunately, in SCO spaces, this issue is not in the limelight as yet. Even in its treaties and agreements, the issue of women empowerment is a shelved one. The biggest challenge in effectively mobilising the participation of women rested on realising the need to ensure their well-being in all areas – physical, psychological, intellectual, emotional, socio-cultural, financial and spiritual.

The SCO leaders and nations must pave the way to introduce new perspectives to give momentum to the drive for women empowerment in a positive direction. Therefore, large-scale joint efforts are needed to deliberate upon the theories of women empowerment – particularly in the SCO context – and draw practical pathways to introduce economic assistance packages by the SCO members, from their state to municipality and individual levels. A whole new subject of 'domestic economy' should be introduced, while promoting the concept of equal burden of care and domestic responsibilities between men and women.

Other than this, special attention must be given to the psychological and spiritual well-being of women, as their responsibilities are manifold. Again, this is where Pakistan's Sufi thoughts, practices, traditions and orientations can help women in SCO spaces to acquire inner peace and function as fully empowered human beings in all spheres of life.

Policy Recommendations

In the light of the debate conducted in the sections above, the following recommendations are given in four different areas:

- Establish an SCO forum on Sufism;
- Create an inter-faith dialogue for brotherhood in the SCO;
    - o Formulate an SCO inter-civilisational dialogue of the modern times for charting a peaceful course of interaction at the civilisational core;
    - o Conduct frequent workshops on creating awareness on women's rights in the SCO and its member countries;
    - o Need for new theories for ensuring women's rights and acknowledging their excellence in every field by all SCO family members;
    - o Need for a separate legal document/treaty/convention on introducing a new paradigm of women's rights from the perspective of spirituality.

Conclusion

This paper briefly discussed the need to 'reconnect' hearts and 'rejuvenate' minds in the SCO spaces by introducing Sufism, cultural and civilisational diplomacy and new dimensions of women empowerment. It revolved around the idea that due to a shared spiritual heritage and the common interests of peace and prosperity for carving a shared destiny, the SCO family has the potential to move beyond the misleading concept of civilisational diversity being a cause for 'clashes' among nations. It also maintained that the SCO would gradually evolve and operationalise an inter-civilisational model of human interactions and foreign relations that can 'reconnect' the SCO nations – even at the levels where one could see issues of disagreement – and 'rejuvenate' the individual legacies. In this regard, this paper was a contribution from Pakistan to enrich the multicultural wisdom and the array of civilisational legacies in the SCO by featuring its various kinds of assets, particularly its Sufi culture.

5

Economic Development Strategy of Shanghai Cooperation Organisation and Security Issues of Further Development

Saidmurodov Lyutfillo

The key message of our conference is that as the SCO grows in strength, so do the challenges that it faces. Without delving into the discussion about the world order that is being formed nowadays, it may be noted that the issues of the economic component in the activities of the SCO today are no less important than political, military and humanitarian ones. The security of the further development of the SCO is definitely largely associated with the need to form an economic doctrine within the integrated space of this organisation.

As is known, the SCO pays great attention to economic cooperation. Over the past decades, the SCO has managed to build one of the world's largest systems of regional interaction, with an emphasis on guaranteeing political stability, strengthening security and expanding trade and economic cooperation.

The interaction mechanisms and formats of cooperation created within the framework of the SCO provide a unique opportunity to combine the national interests of each member state with the interests of the development of the SCO region. At the same time, the fundamental changes that the entire system of international relations, including economic ones, are currently experiencing, dictate the need for the development of a joint economic development strategy for the SCO region that meets the challenges and threats of our time.

The SCO has developed a solid contractual and legal framework and has accumulated significant economic and investment potential, which makes a significant contribution to improving trade and economic cooperation in the region. The Programme of Multilateral Trade and Economic Cooperation of the SCO member states and the action plan for its consistent implementation contribute to the expansion and strengthening of cooperation in finance, investment, industry, transport, energy, agriculture and other fields and is in the interests of sustainable socio-economic development in the SCO region.

After the COVID-19 pandemic, which became the biggest shock of the beginning of the 21st century and presented new challenges and threats, the global economy entered a qualitatively new period of recovery growth, accompanied by a high level of economic and political volatility. In our opinion, for the SCO, the new conditions of world development dictate the need to search for non-standard answers to key international challenges.

The fact is that the current global fundamental processes are accompanied by the strengthening of multipolarity and the system of global economic regulation is undergoing a process of reformatting. Existing multilateral economic partnerships are being reviewed and new ones are being created. Established supply chains are being disrupted. The sphere of economy is being liberalised and has become a weapon in the geopolitical struggle. The policy of sanctions and restrictions on the access to finance are becoming the rule rather than the exception. The world economy is experiencing uncertainty and instability due to risks and crises. Alternative payment systems are emerging. The global prices of raw materials fluctuate frequently. Unemployment is increasing and consumer demand is declining. These and many other factors exacerbate the instability and uncertainty in the global economy and create additional challenges for economic growth and ensuring social well-being as well as food security in the SCO space.

Under these conditions, new approaches are required to promote more equitable and efficient international cooperation and sustainable economic development. Today, the SCO is a comprehensive trans-regional organisation with the largest territory and population in the world, rich resources and huge potential, which determine its special obligations to the world community. Therefore, the synergy of the economic potential of the SCO member states can give a win-win result. The successful development of each SCO member state will steadily contribute to the sustainable development of all partners and, ultimately, serve as the basis for the prosperity of the common Eurasian space.

The emerging new economic conditions in the world dictate an urgent need to search for and find non-standard approaches to the formation of the most effective model of trade and economic cooperation within the SCO, thereby expanding ties with traditional and new partners. At the same time, the 'green agenda' is invariably kept within the focus of the increased attention of the SCO countries. In 2021, the Green Belt Programme of the SCO was adopted, which emphasised the need to further strengthen cooperation in the field of green and sustainable development.

The President of the Republic of Tajikistan, the esteemed Emomali Rahmon, took the initiative to prepare the SCO Economic Development Strategy for the period until 2030, which can be an expected response to the key international challenges facing this organisation. Tajikistan has already prepared a draft of this strategy and it is under active discussion by the SCO member states.

Like many other projects of the SCO, the SCO Economic Development Strategy for the period up to 2030 should reflect the coordinated views and common vision of the SCO space states, in the direction of expanding economic cooperation, coordinating and 'pairing' national strategies and multilateral projects, in terms of sustainable development in the medium-term.

An important feature of the project is that, based on the general principles of the functioning of the SCO, i.e., mutual respect for sovereignty, equality of all member states, the gradual implementation of joint actions in areas of common interest, the prevention of any illegal actions directed against the interests of the SCO and non-orientation of the SCO against other states and international organisations, it determines the trajectory of the medium-term economic development of the SCO, on the basis of four particular principles:

- **The principle of prevention,** which implies coordinated preventive actions aimed at reducing the vulnerability of the national economies of the SCO states to external shocks.
- **The principle of priority,** which determines coordinated actions, primarily in the interests of multilateral economic cooperation.
- **The principle of security,** concentrating on the consistency of actions in the areas of energy, food and technogenic, environmental and information security.
- **The principle of 'green development',** directing joint efforts to increase economic growth rates with minimal impact on the environment.

Of course, the key goal of the strategy is to create favourable conditions for effective cooperation and ensure a strategic breakthrough of the SCO in the economic sphere, aimed at improving the level and quality of life of the citizens of the SCO states. At the same time, the project also defines the strategic goal of the economic development of the SCO countries in the medium-term. This includes the formation of the pre-requisites for the gradual implementation of the free movement of goods, capital, services and technologies, including 'green' and low-emission technologies in the SCO space, as provided for in the charter and the Green Belt programme of the organisation. Nevertheless, the project also defines its operational goals, the achievement of which is associated with the formation of stable, transparent and simplified rules and procedures in the field of trade, banking and finance and investment between interested SCO member states as well as the activation of mutually beneficial bilateral and multilateral cooperation and the exchange of experience in the use and implementation of 'green' and low-emission technologies.

According to forecasts, the global economic processes in the future will be characterised by increased uncertainty, with possible changes under the influence of geopolitical factors and the growth of protectionism, including in the form of unilateral restrictions on trade.

Therefore, in our opinion, in view of the difficult situation in the world, the priorities of multilateral economic cooperation of the SCO member states should be aimed at counteracting the emerging economic challenges. It is clear that if concerted preventive adaptation measures are not taken, these challenges can turn into serious threats.

From these positions, it is important to emphasise that the intensification of cooperation between the SCO member countries in the trade, economic, technological and financial spheres is becoming the main priority in the aspect of ensuring security and 'green development' in the medium term and the further integration of the SCO into the modern world architecture of international relations.

In our opinion, these goals, principles and priorities of the strategy are focused on realising the potential of the SCO in the direction of strengthening it as a comprehensive trans-regional organisation in the modern world and even greater involvement of it in the architecture of international economic relations.

Therefore, there is an academic endeavour on our part aimed at finding ways to expand cooperation in the field of sustainable and balanced development of territories, implement joint projects, exchange experience and best practices and develop agreed-upon approaches in the development of an open, transparent, inclusive and non-discriminatory international trading system.

Based on the foregoing, the following can be identified as the main areas of action within the framework of the established priorities of the strategy aimed at ensuring the security of further development:

- **In the field of cooperation in the trade sphere:** Improving the quality of trade; ensuring the security and stability of the international production and supply chain.
- **In the field of cooperation directly in the economic sphere:** Coordination of efforts to ensure energy and food security; development of digital and 'green' economy.
- **In the field of cooperation in the technological sphere:** Development and implementation of projects for investment cooperation and industrial cooperation; exchange of experience in the field of 'green' design.
- **In the field of cooperation in the financial sector:** Formation of mechanisms for the financial support of the SCO's project activities; development of a system of cross-border 'green' financial instruments.

Notes

1. "Program of multilateral trade and economic cooperation of the member states of the Shanghai Cooperation Organisation". Approved by the Decision of the Council of Heads of Government (Prime Ministers) of the Member States of the Shanghai Cooperation Organisation dated September 23, 2003, No. 1.
2. "Qingdao Declaration of the Council of Heads of State of the Shanghai Cooperation Organisation". URL: http://kremlin.ru/supplement/5315
3. "Development Strategy of the Shanghai Cooperation Organization until 2025". Approved by the Decision of the Council of Heads of State of the Shanghai Cooperation Organization, No. 1, dated July 10, 2015.
4. "Green Belt Program of the Shanghai Cooperation Organization". Approved by the Decision of the Council of Heads of State of the Shanghai Cooperation Organization, No. 9, dated September 17, 2021.
5. Nurlanova, N.K., "Central Asia: New Opportunities and Architecture for Building National Economies". // *Journal of Economic Reforms,* 2018, No. 1 (29).

6

SCO and Uzbekistan

Batyr Tursunov

Today, we are witnessing cardinal changes as a result of the systemic transformation of the modern world order. Traditional and new challenges and threats to international security have increased. There is a lack of trust and mutual understanding. Geopolitical turbulence has intensified as never before, which is aggravating the economic, energy and environmental crisis. The world has entered a dangerous period of strategic tension, uncertainty and unpredictability. This trend is increasingly reflected in the stability in the SCO space.

In these difficult conditions, the SCO countries need to pay special attention to the following fundamentally important issues. First, the SCO should continue to adhere to the principle of non-alignment. Openness to constructive dialogue and international cooperation is a key condition for the effectiveness and attractiveness of our organisation.

Secondly, the SCO states need to remain committed to the principle of consensus as a factor of equal and mutually beneficial cooperation, based on the consideration of mutual interests.

Third, the SCO family is expanding, but Central Asia should remain its 'geographical core' as it is located in the heart of the vast Eurasia.

In our opinion, the effectiveness of the SCO will be determined by active cooperation in the following fields:

Transport Connectivity

The vast space of the SCO, which today also covers the Middle East, has huge transport and transit potential. Certainly, its implementation will create new opportunities for giving a powerful impetus to the development and prosperity of the countries of the big SCO family. In this regard, this task is a strategic imperative.

Today, the SCO countries are actively involved in the implementation of transport projects designed to link the major markets of the Asia-Pacific region, Europe, the Middle East and Central and South Asia. It is critically important to form a diversified system of transport and transit communications along the East-West and North-South axes.

During the Samarkand SCO Summit in September 2022, a trilateral agreement was signed to start the China-Kyrgyzstan-Uzbekistan railway construction project. This is a historic event that is designed to increase the geoeconomic potential, not only of Central Asia, but also of the entire SCO region.

Another strategically important project is the construction of the Trans-Afghan Railway on the Termez-Mazar-i-Sharif-Kabul-Peshawar route. The implementation of these two projects will open up wide opportunities for strengthening connectivity, increasing trade and investment and promoting economic growth in the SCO space.

The reasons behind the construction of the Trans-Afghan Railway are:

- To realise the transit potential of the regions of Central and South Asia
- To form the shortest route, significantly reducing the time and costs of cargo transportation
- To create a modern transport and logistics infrastructure that will connect Central and South Asia

It should be noted that the first cargo from Uzbekistan arrived in Peshawar via this route, in November 2021. In March 2022, India, for the first time, exported its goods to Uzbekistan via Pakistani and Afghan territory on the Mumbai-Karachi-Kabul route.

Moreover, the Trans-Afghan Corridor is intended to become a new route, along with the existing corridors, to the ports of Chabahar and Bandar Abbas, for the access of the Central Asian countries to the seaports of Karachi and Gwadar.

The construction of the Trans-Afghan Highway should be considered as a part of the efforts to achieve peace, security and development in Afghanistan. It is obvious that the implementation of this project will reduce the time and cost of cargo transportation between the countries of South Asia and Europe through Central Asia.

This initiative, along with such projects as the Surkhan-Pul-i-Khumri power line, CASA-1000 and TAPI gas pipeline, can trigger the economic development of all the countries of Central and South Asia.

Naturally, Afghanistan will become one of the major beneficiaries of such connectivity projects, linking the North-South and East-West routes. Due to its geographical location, Afghanistan should become a strategic hub connecting the countries of Central Asia and South Asia. This will open up huge prospects, not only for the countries of the two regions, including Pakistan and India, but also for the entire vast Eurasia.

Economy, Trade and Investment

Cooperation in these areas requires increased practical investment. This is one of the key conditions for ensuring stability, development and prosperity. At the SCO Samarkand Summit, President Shavkat Mirziyoyev proposed using reliable models of regional cooperation to achieve greater economic sustainability. It is necessary to move on to real actions to build production chains with a shorter 'supply shoulder'.

It is important to start forming a common space of industrial and technological cooperation based on the launch of a New SCO Economic Dialogue, which provides for:

- The elimination of trade and customs barriers
- The formation of guaranteed and stable production and supply chains
- The promotion of joint localisation and import substitution programmes
- The promotion of mutual investments in the development of infrastructure, industry and the service sector

The issues of cooperation in the field of food security require special attention. Our countries have sufficient potential. In this regard, it is necessary to develop general principles and approaches for ensuring food security. At the same time, it is important to provide for specific measures to bring the regulatory framework closer, conduct joint research and introduce innovations.

Security Challenges and Threats

Radicalism, extremism and terrorism remain key challenges to security and stability in the SCO space. The powerful progress of information technology has transformed these challenges into more serious threats that require active systemic cooperation within the SCO.

First, it is important to strengthen the coordination of the activities of law enforcement agencies and special services of the SCO countries.

Secondly, it is necessary to increase the effectiveness of the SCO Regional Anti-Terrorist Structure (RATS). This includes issues of prevention and prompt response to security challenges and threats.

Thirdly, we consider it expedient to enforce a set of measures aimed at preventing the involvement of young people in extremist organisations thus creating a younger generation of stable immunity to various destructive ideologies.

7

Peace and Prosperity in the SCO Space through Consolidation and Cooperation: View from Belarus

Oleg Makarov

Abstract

The views of the Belarusian side on the consequences of the global turn towards the SCO for the politics, security and economy of the region are described in this paper. The latter deals with the vision of ways to achieve peace and prosperity (SCO responses) against the backdrop of ongoing geopolitical shifts and also includes a discussion on the contours of the 'road map' for increasing stability in Eurasia and the SCO space through expert diplomacy.

It is symbolic that a historic event may take place in the two months that Belarus is here in the ancient but eternally young Delhi, in the land of Gandhi and the Buddha – it will likely become a full member of the SCO family. Therefore, an attempt is made to firstly, assess the role and place of the SCO in the context of the global 'Pivot to East and South'; secondly, outline the vision of associated risks and challenges; and, in conclusion, outline the contours of the 'road map' for the expert and analytical community of the SCO through the prism of the Belarusian experience.

Today, the shift of the global focus to the East and South is already obvious to almost everyone. Both sub-regions confidently occupy strong positions in the emerging world order. It is this part of the planet that is the 'heart' of the world, a source of energy, trade, population and other resources. The world will never return to its former normality. The point of no return has been passed.

Against the background of such a planetary shift, the SCO is becoming the 'designer' of a new, more just architecture of a polycentric world order, a community of like-minded states striving sovereignly, without dictate, blackmail and external threats, to determine their own path of development and image of the future.

Due to the consonance of the principles of the SCO with the main provisions of the foreign policy of our country, Belarus made a conscious choice, back in 2010, in favour of this association. This position was confirmed during a recent meeting in Minsk between President A. Lukashenko and SCO Secretary General Zhang Ming.

Naturally, the path to international recognition, peace and prosperity is not easy. It is thorny, especially against the backdrop of today's geopolitical shifts and turbulence.

The coronavirus pandemic has exacerbated the problems of hunger, poverty and access to public health. Well-established supply chains as well as the usual schemes of financial settlements have been disrupted or broken. National self-centeredness and unfair competition are growing, which leads to a decrease in mutual trust and exacerbates the debt crisis.

Climate change is causing natural disasters. Technogenic disasters are not inferior in the severity of their destructive consequences, as they often become the result of deliberate and malicious influence from outside. The lack of cohesion in the use of water resources leads to their shortage and the growth of contradictions.

Despite all the advantages of expansion in the SCO, the institutional challenges remain relevant, as new players inevitably bring both their internal and regional contradictions into the common space.

Main Challenges and Risks

Militarisation of the global space: This is because of the shift in the global focus from the concept of development to security. The response of the SCO, as a balancer, may be an alternative responsible approach to 'security through development', achieving a multiple excess of the speed of sustainable development processes over the dynamics of challenges and threats.

Regionalisation as an alternative to the globalisation project: The pros and cons of this new reality have yet to be assessed. However, due to varying degrees of internal readiness for integration, this is a serious challenge for many, which is based on the growing competition and rivalry for resources. The balance between respect for the national sovereignty of the states and proper governance is also important, which can be ensured by borrowing the best world integration practices. The SCO's answer here can be the formula of 'Peace, Connectivity and Development'.

Deterioration of general living conditions in the world: This is due to climate change, increased threats to biological and environmental security and a decrease in the quality of environmental protection as well as the level of access to health care. The SCO's answer is to develop its own thematic agenda, free from national egoism and excessive commercialisation, including on the basis of scientifically based approaches and mechanisms.

Technological imbalances: These are both natural and artificial and are caused by the arbitrary and unjustified illegitimate restrictive measures of external players, which are aimed at curbing the development of individual states. The SCO's response is to move from a "race for leadership" to closer cooperation in order to create unique Eurasian technologies based on respect for each other's technological sovereignty and building a non-discriminatory system for their transfer and a core market with country specialisation. In addition, it is important to radically revise the system of financing education and science, which should be focused on solving purely internal common tasks and problems.

Resource endowment: Although Eurasia is self-sufficient in terms of the availability of basic resources, externally imposed extraction patterns and supply chains lead to their uncontrolled scouring. The answer of the SCO to this issue is the creation of a closed resource ecosystem that will be based on internal cooperation, conscientious interaction with partners and fair, transparent and reasonable distribution in proportion to real needs, possibly with the regulation of these processes at the supranational level.

Demographic (generational) gap: Although this challenge manifests itself in different ways, it is common to many countries. It is obvious that the current generation of young people is uncomfortable within the framework proposed (especially imposed) by the older generation, regardless of nation and religion. The net effect of the 'fermentation' of young minds is a long-term challenge that, if moderated externally, can become a real threat to national security. The SCO's answer is the formation of an attractive image of the Eurasian future, which will captivate and inspire, creating social lifts that are so necessary for self-realisation. It is believed that the concept, "The SCO space is a common home", with equal conditions and opportunities for all, is appropriate for the young people.

In this regard, the experience of the Union State of Russia and Belarus can become an example of effective integration for the SCO.

We are convinced that the formation of an image of the future is conceptually important from the point of view of goal-setting for the development of the SCO. Although its horizon is not clearly visible today due to the fog of military conflicts, analysts should strive to see peaceful contours behind this veil and based on this vision, build long-term plans for creation and development. If not, we run the risk of running into a dead end at the next round of turbulence, for which there are many examples in history.

It is natural that the main competition in the world revolves around the design of the image of the future. In our opinion, this area is the main task and a challenge for the SCO expert community.

As part of solving this problem, the Belarusian Institute of Strategic Research (BISR)developed a methodology in 2020, based on the best practices of identifying, substantiating and predicting global trends in direct correlation with the national interests of Belarus. The result of this work was the analytical report, "The image of the future of Belarus in the context of global trends". We are ready to bring these and other progressive developments as our practical contributions to strengthening the expert and analytical basis of the SCO.

We are convinced that the SCO needs a set of unifying ideas. For example, the basis can be the fight against poverty (with the development of clear and specific indicators), inflation, unfair distribution of benefits and the debt crisis, the creation of an effective ecosystem of mutual trade, logistics and finance, exchange of best practices, etc.

One thing is clear: the SCO space is not a place for conflicts and wars.

Expert diplomacy is an important tool for deepening regional integration in the SCO space and jointly responding to modern risks and challenges. Previously, ideas were repeatedly expressed regarding the establishment of more systematic and coordinated expert work in the SCO. This concerns the SCO Forum as an international network of national scientific, expert and analytical centres.

In 2020, at the height of the coronavirus pandemic, the launch of the world's first Inter-Party Expert Group (IPEG) was announced at the forum of the leading parliamentary parties of the countries participating in the SCO family (SCO+).

In September 2022, Tashkent hosted the first Scientific and Expert Forum of the SCO on Information Security, organised by the Institute for Strategic and Regional Studies under the President of the Republic of

Uzbekistan, together with the Executive Committee of the RATS, SCO. It is certain that expert diplomacy, due to its creative potential, can play one of the leading roles in the search for answers to the existing challenges.

Therefore, we strongly support the idea of a permanent expert dialogue in the SCO, which will make it possible to establish stable ties between think-tanks, increase the level of mutual trust and understanding and also make a significant contribution to the formation of a common market of ideas and an image of the future of Eurasia.

We are interested in the comprehensive involvement of the scientific and educational institutions of the countries of the SCO Forum in the interests of developing scientific oriental research in Belarus, including the development of specialised educational programmes.

Undoubtedly, given the impending promotion of the status of our country in the SCO, the accession of the BISR to the mechanism of the SCO Forum is a matter of time and will only increase the dynamics, scope and practical impact of such an interaction.

An international conference in Minsk, with the participation of high representatives of the CSTO member states, the SCO, the UN and other international organisations, on the issues of Eurasian security, with an emphasis on the interdependence of the issues of sustainable development and sustainable security, can be a convenient platform for discussing these and other topical issues.

In conclusion, the Republic of Belarus intends to continue to make its constructive and active contribution to the progressive development of the SCO space and ensure stability, security and prosperity in the region. There is no doubt that only by truly uniting and rallying, will we be able to ensure the safe revival and rejuvenation of Eurasia as well as its sustainable development for the future generations.

8

Reconnecting the People: Mongolia's Participation in the SCO

Soyolgerel Nyamjav

Abstract

Mongolia has stated in its strategic documents, namely, the Foreign Policy Concept and the National Security Concept, that it will "maintain balanced relations and develop broad-based good-neighbourly cooperation with its two neighbours, expand friendly relations and cooperation with developed countries" and support policies and activities aimed at strengthening strategic stability and expanding security cooperation in Northeast and Central Asia. These constitute the basis of Mongolia's policy of relations with the SCO.

Over the past two decades, the SCO's heft and influence in the region have been growing and expanding. Mongolia has been an active observer of the SCO since 2004, when it became its first observer state. This presentation seeks to discuss Mongolia's participation in the SCO and how the researchers view the organisation's development and prospects.

Development Prospects of the SCO in the Near Future

The main goals of the SCO are to strengthen mutual trust and good-neighbourly relations among its members, promote effective cooperation in the political, trade, economic and cultural spheres, establish a new and democratic international order in the region and collectively strive for peace, security and stability.

Its members understand that non-alignment, avoidance of extremism and openness are the principles of the SCO's foreign policy. Political, security, economic, cultural and humanitarian cooperation is identified as a priority and the SCO members agree that economic cooperation is the weakest of these.

Much attention is paid to maintaining security and stability in the region. The Moscow Declaration, adopted at the end of the 2020 Summit, is an important document that reflects the key issues that the SCO will pay attention to in the future. The declaration states that member states are committed to strengthening foreign policy coherence in the international arena, maintaining global stability and existing mechanisms governing arms control and intensifying cooperation in the fight against international terrorism.

These key issues include:

- Combating the pandemic
- Ensuring security in the SCO space
- Developing inter-parliamentary and inter-judiciary relations
- Intensifying trade and economic cooperation
- Development of cultural and humanitarian exchanges
- Active participation in the international arena and in multilateral cooperation organisations.

The legal framework for the SCO to achieve these goals is relatively well-established. To date, more than 100 documents regulating the activities of various sectors of cooperation have been approved.

Mongolia's Participation in the SCO

Mongolia has a unique geographical location as it is part of both Northeast Asia and Central Asia and active participation in the multilateral political and economic processes taking place in these regions is an important part of its foreign policy. Therefore, in 2004, Mongolia was granted observer status in the SCO, recognising it as an important channel for multilateral cooperation in the Central Asian region. During the discussion of the issue of observer status in the SCO by the National Security Council, it was recommended to increase participation in economic cooperation within the SCO, in particular, in the areas of energy, infrastructure and transit transport. Since gaining observer status, Mongolia has been regularly participating in the SCO Summit of Heads of State and Government.

Mongolia is more interested in participating in economic cooperation within the SCO, including in the areas of energy, infrastructure and transit transport. The country expressed interest in implementing projects within the SCO, such as connecting the western part of Mongolia with the Central

Asian countries, establishing a free trade zone in the Bayan-Ulgii province and transferring energy projects between Russia and China through Mongolia as well as talks between the SCO member states. It also expressed interest in participating in specific projects, such as the opening of a continental transport corridor between the North and South and Asia and Europe and the establishment of a SCO food security cooperation mechanism. Mongolia has focused on the implementation of the SCO Multilateral Trade and Economic Cooperation Programme and has proposed the development of a similar programme with the participation of members, observers and dialogue partners.

Over the past years, Mongolia has taken specific initiatives to strengthen the SCO observer status, enhance the rights and responsibilities of the observers and deepen cooperation between the observers and member states. Numerous SCO documents and speeches by the SCO leaders and SCO Secretaries-General emphasise the importance of expanding cooperation with observer countries and making better use of their resources, indicating that our efforts have played an important role.

Mongolia was the first observer state to invite and host the visit of the SCO Secretary General in 2007. The 2010 SCO Business Council meeting in Ulaanbaatar was the first of its kind in an observer country. The meeting helped to strengthen business ties between member and observer countries and provide our private sector with more information on the activities of the SCO and economic cooperation within the organisation.

Over the past years, our country has participated in and hosted a plethora of SCO events and put forth certain initiatives to expand cooperation, but has not been able to participate in specific economic projects and programmes of utmost interest to us within the SCO. This is primarily due to the low level of economic cooperation within the SCO. On the other hand, it is also due to the fact that our country has not made specific proposals, based on calculations and research, for cooperation in the areas of its interest.

The relevant ministries and organisations in Mongolia probably do not conduct research on the SCO and do not have staff in charge of relations with the organisation. Hence, the possibility of developing specific cooperation proposals and projects has been limited.

As Mongolia has not been involved in any economic projects or programmes, it can be concluded that it has not benefitted from the SCO's activities in the past. However, its observer status in the SCO can be considered politically significant. The SCO has given us a platform to express our interests in cooperation within the Central Asian region. During Mongolia's participation in the summits, its leaders held bilateral meetings with the leaders of the SCO member and observer states, which helped to develop cooperation with those countries. Becoming an observer was important to gain insight into the ongoing cooperation within the SCO, which is playing an increasingly important role in regional affairs and the policies and activities of member and observer states.

Mongolia is more interested in participating in economic cooperation within the SCO, including in the areas of energy, infrastructure and transit transport. Moreover, the SCO should pay more attention to the economic cooperation of its member states and adhere to the pragmatic principle that not all countries participate in any economic project and that all interested countries should implement it jointly.

Mongolia is also interested in implementing projects, such as the renovation of the Mongolian railway connecting Russia and China and the construction of a railway and road connecting the western part of Mongolia with Central Asia, as SCO projects. The SCO member states and observer states have always stressed the importance of conducting joint exercises, providing protection against natural disasters that cover a large area of the region and cause the loss of lives and property.

In order to increase the effectiveness of its participation in the SCO, Mongolia needs to develop and follow a detailed SCO policy. It should classify the areas of involvement in the SCO as prioritised areas of participation (economic cooperation, such as energy, infrastructure, transit transport, agriculture), areas of active participation (education, culture, science, health, environment, disaster management) and appropriate areas for participation (combating terrorism, drugs and narcotics) and the relevant agencies need to be actively involved in these activities.

The main condition for increasing the real outcome of our participation is to prepare and propose to relevant parties, the specific projects and programmes that can be implemented bilaterally and multilaterally within the SCO. Among the agreements signed within the SCO, it is necessary to study the possibility of joining some of those that are important for our country.

In addition to government agencies, the role of the private sector and academia is important in making Mongolia's participation in the SCO more effective. The regular and active participation of our relevant organisations in the activities of the three non-governmental structures within the SCO, such as the Business Council, the Banking Consortium and the SCO Forum, will help to increase Mongolia's participation and improve its results.

Scientists and researchers from the SCO member states should exchange views on the organisation's activities and actively participate in the activities of the SCO Forum, which is the main channel for making suggestions and recommendations to government agencies.

There is a need to establish a research centre or an informal council on the SCO, based on one or two home-based research institutions. The Mongolian National Chamber of Commerce and Industry's involvement in the Business Council needs to be made permanent. In addition, our banks need to be involved, as appropriate, in the activities of the Banking Consortium.

Trade and Economic Relations between the SCO Members and Mongolia: Current State and Trends

Trade between the SCO countries (excluding Russia and China) and Mongolia amounted to US$ 93.2 million in 2021, which is less than 1 percent of Mongolia's total foreign trade turnover. In terms of investment, with the exception of Russia and China, the SCO members are investing less in Mongolia. However, one shall not deny a small amount of investment, in meat and cashmere processing, from Kazakhstan, Uzbekistan, India and Pakistan. With the exception of the investment of US$ 1 billion by India's Exim Bank in the Sainshand oil refinery, there has been no inter-governmental relationship with the SCO in the form of soft loans and grants.

Conclusion

Mongolia has been a regular observer of the SCO as part of its policy of active participation in regional political and economic cooperation and is interested in further cooperation with the organisation. We believe that there is great potential for mutually beneficial cooperation with the SCO member states and observers in developing mutually beneficial economic cooperation to ensure regional security.

9

Integration Toolkit for Regional Countries: View from Armenia[i]

Gohar Iskandaryan

The bipolar world order, formed after World War II, underwent a transformative shift towards a unipolar structure after the collapse of the USSR. It became increasingly evident that this new format did not fit the interests of the developing countries. The search for new solutions became imperative.

On June 15, 2001, Kazakhstan, Kyrgyzstan, China, Russia, Tajikistan and Uzbekistan founded the Shanghai Cooperation Organisation (SCO) in Shanghai. This essentially constituted one of the directions of that solution.

The main goal of the SCO has been to develop political, economic (trade), technological (scientific) and cultural relations between the member states, in an environment of mutual trust as well as to advance cooperation between them in the energy, transport, tourism, environmental protection and other sectors. The members should join efforts to fight against terrorism, separatism and extremism and contribute to the joint provision and maintenance of peace, security and stability in the region.[1]

Although India was not a founding member of the SCO, the programmes implemented by New Delhi, in 2012, coincided with the ideas of the SCO. In 2012, India implemented the 'Connect Central Asia' policy.[2] The term 'Global South' came to the fore. This term summed up the interests of the

i The work was supported by the Science Committee of RA, in the frames of the research project № 21T-5F218.

Far East countries with their positions and roles. In 2017, India joined the SCO. This move obviously increased the weight of SCO.

In 2005, Iran received observer status and after studying the opportunities offered by the organisation over the years, it ultimately concluded that the policy adopted by the SCO corresponds to Iran's policy towards the region. 15 years later, in September 2021, Iran's application to become a full member of the organisation was accepted.[3] In 2022, Iran signed a memorandum in Samarkand, expressing its desire to become a full member of the SCO.[4] This will amplify the efforts aimed at the security system of the structure as well as create new opportunities for the activation of cultural ties.

In fact, within a considerably short timeline, the SCO succeeded in including almost all the powerful countries of the Far East and many others have observer status. Thus, the SCO has great potential to expand and include the countries of the region, thereby contributing to their development. Nevertheless, it is important to acknowledge that the interests of the influential regional powers may not always align harmoniously. It is necessary to have determination and patience and to remain faithful to the spirit of the SCO in an atmosphere of tolerance. It may be emphasised that in order for the SCO structure to combine multiple interests and have seamlessly working mechanisms, it is necessary to develop relations between the member and observer countries on both micro and macro levels.

In this article, the role and position of Armenia in the SCO as well as the problems and challenges related to it have been discussed.

In 2016, Armenia received the status of a 'dialogue partner' in the SCO. During the signing ceremony, the Secretary General of the SCO emphasised that it is gratifying to include a country with an ancient history like Armenia in the SCO family.[5]

Armenia, as an ancient nation, has a rich institutional history of centuries-long cooperation with both India and Iran. Additionally, it is worth highlighting that Armenia, Iran and India share a geographical proximity, which historically facilitated easier collaboration among them. At the same time, Armenia, as a member of the former Soviet Union, has a 70-year experience of cooperation, established relations and understanding of the issues at hand with the former Soviet countries, since it has the experience of understanding the mentality and values. Moreover, we should note that Armenia is perhaps the only country operating within the framework of the SCO, which has local Armenian communities and diaspora representatives in almost all the SCO member countries. So, Armenia has great potential for cooperation. This is a very important factor, which, if used correctly, can contribute to the regional development of the SCO and under no circumstances should this be considered secondary.

In addition, from the political perspective, Russia is Armenia's strategic ally and Iran is Armenia's natural ally. Armenia has warm relations with India, with regular consultations in the political sphere. Having all this on its plate, it becomes obvious how Armenia can make this micro-system work, especially by having the status of a dialogue partner in the SCO and essentially striving for the status of an observer country.

Perhaps, the most important aspect that catches our attention in the list of SCO partnerships is the launch of transportation projects, which are gaining momentum in the region, in the 21st century. The International North-South Transport Corridor (INSTC) project is one such important venture, which holds considerable significance for India, Iran, Russia and even more so, for Armenia. The length of the transport project is about 7,200 km. Armenia, Azerbaijan, Belarus, Kazakhstan, Oman and Syria applied to join the agreement. Armenia joined the Inter-governmental Agreement on the 'North-South International Transport Corridor' on April 13, 2006.

The reference to the North-South programme by the second president of Armenia, Robert Kocharyan, is noteworthy: "At that time, there was no such activity on the Russian side either... It was important for us to shift at least several cargo shipment routes to pass through Armenia... Without the railway, it is difficult to imagine the importance of North-South for Armenia."[6]

The third president of Armenia, Serzh Sargsyan, highlighted this important transport link and suggested paying attention to the Armenia-Iran railway construction project. Emphasising the possibility of Armenia's participation in the aforementioned economic projects, President Serzh Sargsyan added: "In the case of Armenia, such a project can be the construction of the Armenia-Iran railway, which will provide access to the EAEU (Eurasian Economic Union) countries to the Indian Ocean through the Persian Gulf."[7] All this shows that the North-South corridor programme has been very important for the Armenian leadership at all times.

Nonetheless, the progress of the implementation of the programme encountered obstacles and experienced delays owing to a combination of objective and subjective factors. Notably, a significant hindrance to the project's advancement was the imposition of sanctions by the United Nations Security Council on Iran. It is remarkable that India-Iran cooperation intensified in 2015, when the Iranian authorities signed the nuclear agreement in Vienna. Following these developments, New Delhi, recognising the potential opportunities arising from an engagement with

Iran, promptly emerged as one of the early adopters in seeking to strengthen its cooperation with Tehran. It would not only solve India's energy security problems through Iranian hydrocarbon resources, but India would also have access to Central Asian markets through both Russia and Iran. In order to put all this on a more constructive basis, Indian Prime Minister Narendra Modi visited Iran in 2016. The main objective of the visit was to conclude a trilateral agreement between Iran, India and Afghanistan, under which the transit corridor would be used. This entailed the use of the Iranian port of Chabahar. The road was supposed to pass in the direction of Chabahar-Zahedan-Zaranj. This would allow Afghanistan to directly access the sea through this road and also open India to Central Asia.[8] This was a part of the North-South road, a project that was very important for India.

The other part of the North-South road was expected to pass through Iran, Azerbaijan and Russia, with an alternative road passing through Iran, Armenia and Georgia to Europe. Basically, this important North-South Corridor would also relieve the load of the Suez Canal and contribute to the development of other countries in the region.

To facilitate the construction of the road, the Armenian authorities have actively initiated efforts to seek potential donors. From its inception, the project held significant strategic importance, as it aimed to establish vital communication channels with neighbouring countries, thereby unlocking the access to Central Asian and European markets. This, in turn, would foster economic development and growth for all the participating countries involved in the transport project. The Government of Armenia had set a goal to connect the southern border of the country (Meghri) with the northern gate (Bavra).[9] All this essentially corresponds to the letter and spirit of the SCO goals.

The construction of the road commenced in 2012, with an initial timeline envisioning its completion between 2016 and 2018. However, after the United States' unilateral withdrawal from the nuclear deal with Iran, the regional countries exhibited a more cautious approach in implementing these ambitious plans.

Moreover, such large projects can be implemented only in the case of relative regional stability, but two years after the Artsakh (Nagorno-Karabakh) war of 2020,[10] Azerbaijan's military actions created obstacles both in terms of security and mobility.[11] Moreover, during the Artsakh war, certain actions created security situation, which were unprecedented for our region. These were recorded by the Russian,[12] Iranian[13] and Western[14] partners.

Due to the emergence of security problems, a number of programmes agreed between the SCO member countries in the economic, energy, transport, tourism, environmental and other fields are essentially at risk.

However, it is noteworthy that in October 2021, Indian Foreign Minister Subramanyam Jaishankar strongly emphasised the possibility of deepening Armenia-India relations and the launch of the North-South Road project, passing through India, Iran, Armenia and Georgia.[15] This gave a new impetus for the resumption of work in this direction.

In August 2022, the Minister of Road Construction and Urban Development of Iran, Rostam Ghasemi, expressed the desire to sign a long-term contract with India. In turn, the Minister of Ports, Shipping and Waterways of India stated that "they aim to develop economic relations with Iran through this [Chabahar] port and they hope that the two countries will transform the Chabahar strategic port into one of the most important ports in the world."[16]

It is noteworthy that the construction of the North-South road, which was essentially suspended in Armenia since 2018, resumed in 2021, after the official visits and announcements of the foreign ministers of India and Iran. In 2022, Iranian Foreign Minister Abdollahian stressed on the project of connecting the Persian Gulf to the Black Sea and during his visit to Armenia, noted the following: "We can realise our goals related to this road and play a more important role in the construction of this corridor."

In order to implement this project, the Ministry of Foreign Affairs of Armenia held and participated in more than five offline and online discussions, in order to negotiate the draft agreement on " The establishment of the international transport corridor from the Persian Gulf to the Black Sea". The recent fifth meeting hosted delegations of the Republic of Armenia, the Republic of Bulgaria, Georgia, the Republic of Greece and the Islamic Republic of Iran.[17]

The above-mentioned projects stem from the SCO's goals and principles. Today, Armenia is doing its best to deepen its relations with the SCO. The SCO Secretary General, Zhang Ming, also talked about this in 2022, noting that "SCO member countries are studying the possibility of granting Armenia the status of becoming an observer country and in this regard, I am personally optimistic."[18]

For this article, an interview with the Ambassador of Iran to Armenia, Abbas Badakhshyan Zohuri, was conducted. To the question, "Is the passage of the North-South transport route through Armenia important for Iran?", Ambassador Zohuri responded, "The answer to this question is obvious. The North-South route through Armenia is very important for Iran. We consider the implementation of this project to be an effective step towards increasing the security of the region, promoting trade relations between Iran and Armenia as well as improving the positions of Iran and Armenia in the international communication channels, especially in the section stretching from the Indian Ocean to the Black Sea."[19]

Yerevan has repeatedly stated that the comprehensive deepening and development of relations with India and Iran is one of the priorities of Armenia's foreign policy. On May 30, 2022, the Minister of Foreign Affairs of Armenia, Ararat Mirzoyan, in an interview to an Indian media outlet, Wion, *inter alia* was asked the following question: "On the connectivity front, how do you see projects like the International North-South transport corridor and will you join the Chabahar port project?" The minister replied, "We are actively discussing a number of connectivity projects. In this regard, we are interested in advancing our dialogue and cooperation within the framework of the INSTC project, Chabahar port as well as the Persian Gulf - the Black Sea international transport corridor and we are communicating with other partners on this issue as well. Armenia considers India's potential and prospective role in this corridor to be quite significant. In this sense, we also welcome Indian companies to actively engage in infrastructure projects in Armenia."[20]

On April 26, 2022, Ararat Mirzoyan stated in the framework of his visit to India, "Today, we open a new page in the history of Armenian-Indian economic cooperation and let me say, revive the excellent traditions of trade, development and shared prosperity between our nations."[21] The minister also discussed the project of connecting the Persian Gulf to the Black Sea. This is essentially the restoration of the ancient road between India, Iran and Armenia. This road will contribute to facilitating the export of Indian goods, both to Russia and Europe.

On March 7, 2023, during a meeting with SCO Secretary General Zhang Ming, who arrived in Tehran, the Iranian Deputy Foreign Minister reaffirmed Iran's willingness to play a key role in SCO transport agreements. The organisation's ideas coincide with Iran's regional policy. In this regard, both the Mejlis (Iranian Parliament) and the Council of Guardians of the Constitution have endorsed Iran's membership in the SCO.

In conclusion, it can be asserted that the principles and objectives of the SCO align closely with Armenia's regional vision of fostering sustainable peace and resolving the issue of blocked transport routes. Armenia seeks to further enhance its cooperation with both the organisation as a whole and individual member states in the pursuit of promoting stability within the region, which is inherently fragile. The attainment of these objectives necessitates the implementation of comprehensive macro-programmes that not only align with the overarching macro-programmes of the SCO, but also embody its core ideology.

Moreover, the SCO possesses the required tools to effectively mitigate the escalation of tensions along the Armenia-Azerbaijan contact line, thereby encouraging Azerbaijan to adopt a more constructive approach. By ensuring regional stability, the implementation of numerous economic programmes can be facilitated, fostering the overall development of the entire region.

Notes

1. "Charter of the Shanghai Cooperation Organization", https://www.iri.edu.ar/publicaciones_iri/manual/Doc.%20Manual/Listos%20para%20subir/ASIA/SHANGAI-ORG/charter_shanghai_cooperation_organization.pdf
2. Анурада Ченой, Шанхайская организация сотрудничества и Индия, 27.12.2022, https://ru.valdaiclub.com/a/highlights/shankhayskaya-organizatsiya-sotrudnichestva/
3. Yu.B. Potapov, "Iran and the Shanghai Cooperation Organization: Problems and Prospects of Interaction", Восточный Альманах, выпуск 6, 2022, Политология и История, p. 42.https://dipacademy.ru/documents/5966/%D1%81%D1%82%D0%B0%D1%82%D1%8C%D1%8F_%D0%9F%D0%BE%D1%82%D0%B0%D0%BF%D0%BE%D0%B2.pdf
4. Иран официально вступил в ШОС, Иран подписал меморандум о вступлении в Шанхайскую организацию сотрудничества, 15.09.2022, https://iz.ru/1395690/2022-09-15/iran-ofitcialno-vstupil-v-shos
5. "Armenia was granted a status of dialogue partner in the Shanghai Cooperation Organisation", 16 April, 2016, https://www.mfa.am/en/press-releases/2016/04/16/sco-dial-part/6038
6. "Interview with the Second President of the Republic of Armenia R. Kocharyan", Yerevan, Armenia, 13.03.2023
7. На состоявшемся в Уфе саммите Президент Серж Саргсян выступил с речью, 09.07.2015, https://www.president.am/ru/press-release/item/2015/07/09/President-Serzh-Sargsyan-visit-Russian-Federation/
8. Премьер Индии прибыл в Иран с рабочим визитом, 22.05.2016, https://ria.ru/20160522/1437886016.html
9. 2017 – "Armenia, Road Project, North-South Corridor, section in the northern part of the corridor Yerevan to Abavra", https://collaboration.worldbank.org/content/sites/collaboration-for-development/en/groups/eastern-partnership-transport-panel/documents.entry.html/2017/05/21/2017_-_armenia_road-mpi7.html

10. Andrew S. Bowen, Azerbaijan and Armenia: "The NagornoKarabakh Conflict", *Congressional Research Service*, January 7, 2021, p. 8. https://sgp.fas.org/crs/row/R46651.pdf
11. Thomas de Waal, "Azerbaijan's military action in Armenia has gravely damaged chances of a settlement. EU-mediated negotiations, the only viable peace talks, need greater international support". https://carnegieeurope.eu/strategiceurope/87976?fbclid=IwAR3N4rgsXVu8RkpyaJvbAak3e-AshM4xacvGEY7XP0zng0GGDlAfM3o6xf4
12. В Совбезе России отметили опасность переброски в Нагорный Карабах боевиков из Сирии и Ливии Подробнее в ПГ: https://www.pnp.ru/politics/v-sovbeze-rossii-otmetili-opasnost-perebroski-v-nagornyy-karabakh-boevikov-iz-sirii-i-livii.html
13. Naghsh-e mozduran-e khareji dar monagheshe-e Gharebagh (The role of foreign mercenaries in the Karabakh conflict) (in Persian), http://www.irdiplomacy.ir/fa/news/2000533/%D9%86%D9%82%D8%B4-%D9%85%D8%B2%D8%AF%D9%88%D8%B1%D8%A7%D9%86-%D8%AE%D8%A7%D8%B1%D8%AC%DB%8C-%D8%AF%D8%B1-%D9%85%D9%86%D8%A7%D9%82%D8%B4%D9%87-%D9%82%D8%B1%D9%87-%D8%A8%D8%A7%D8%BA?fbclid=IwAR3Aps78XQHlgmvWLtj2R0ViwaWsEhOyO9koAaWTTN6mrsUOgJIETd3sRDI
14. The UN Working Group on the use of mercenaries said there were widespread reports that the Government of Azerbaijan, with Turkey's assistance, relied on Syrian fighters to shore-up and sustain its military operations in the Nagorno-Karabakh conflict zone, including on the frontline. Mercenaries in and around the Nagorno- Karabakh conflict zone must be withdrawn-UN experts, 11 November, 2020, https://www.ohchr.org/en/press-releases/2020/11/mercenaries-and-around-nagorno-karabakh-conflict-zone-must-be-withdrawn-un?fbclid=IwAR2Ps0LzTJ_rjaaqpqan_oKmWGi0s4zsZzA7I7LjF1d5DIQhURPrsLr9KNc

    John Irish, Michel Rose, "France accuses Turkey of sending Syrian jihadists to Nagorno-Karabakh", https://www.reuters.com/article/us-armenia-azerbaijan-putin-macron-idUSKBN26L3SB?fbclid=IwAR1_AM4l5OYalulg2CPJBdLb2mFUCfg2WAew-1CcgmRcBHLqIR0GKQLB6pA
15. "India, Armenia Agree on Closer Ties", 13.10.2021, https://www.azatutyun.am/a/31507402.html,
16. Иран и Индия продолжают развивать порт Чабахар в Индийском океане, «Каспийский вестник», http://casp-geo.ru/iran-i-indiya-prodolzhayut-razvivat-port-chabahar-v-indijskom-okeane/?fbclid=IwAR22F2GMNaFehIY5g-Fh6jreK1s3cl1hqUMqlJ5JnpwSr9fCH-wIYerqIKg

17. "The expert meeting on Draft Agreement on the Establishment of the Persian Gulf-Black Sea International Transport and Transit Corridor took place at the MFA of the RA", 19 April, 2021, https://www.mfa.am/en/press-releases/2021/04/19/intt/10897
18. ШОС изучает вопрос получения Арменией и Азербайджаном статуса наблюдателя, 24 марта 2022,, https://tass.ru/mezhdunarodnaya-panorama/14166915
19. Interview with the Extraordinary and Plenipotentiary Ambassador of the Republic of Iran to the Republic of Armenia Abbas Badakhshyan Zohuri, Yerevan, Armenia, in electronic version, 12.05.2023
20. Interview of the Foreign Minister of Armenia Ararat Mirzoyan to "WION",30 May, 2022, https://www.mfa.am/en/interviews-articles-and-comments/2022/05/30/Wion_interview/11477
21. "The Armenian-Indian business forum took place", 26 April 2022, https://www.mfa.am/en/speeches/2022/04/26/arm_ind_business/11416

10

A View from Bahrain on the SCO

Abdulrahman Al Gaoud

The Shanghai Cooperation Organisation, as a regional organisation that represents nearly 40 percent of the world's population and more than 20 percent of its GDP, plays a critical role in bringing people together and building bridges of cooperation and collaboration.

The theme of the session speaks to a universal truth that we are all connected and our success as nations and as a global community depends on our ability to work together.

Culture is an essential aspect of the shared heritage of the SCO countries and a source of pride for all. To facilitate the exchange of cultural knowledge and pride as well as promote tourism, education about the life and works of important personalities of the SCO countries should be promoted.

Supporting the development of interfaith dialogue programmes can also be useful in promoting understanding between different religions in the region as well as creating an SCO spiritual tour to promote tourism and the diverse spiritual beliefs and education practices.

Tourism and travel offer an excellent opportunity to promote the shared heritage in the region. Developing a sustainable SCO tourism marketing campaign and facilitating the ease of movement within the region would lead to a greater flow of visitors and appreciation for the attractions in the SCO countries, ultimately benefitting the region's economy and cultural exchange.

It is important to involve the younger generations in preserving the SCO heritage and we can engage them by making heritage accessible and relevant through innovative and interactive approaches, such as incorporating digital technology and social media.

Developing SCO heritage apps, establishing heritage clubs and societies at schools and universities and hosting cultural festivals that showcase the diversity of the SCO heritage, can attract young people and provide them with hands-on experience of traditional arts, crafts and performances.

Assigning young SCO ambassadors or influencers can also help promote and raise awareness of the shared heritage.

We can foster a diverse and vibrant community of heritage advocates by promoting interactions among women, business communities, media, researchers and academicians. Through collaboration and knowledge sharing, we can develop new strategies and ideas to promote and preserve the SCO heritage for the future generations. This can be achieved by organising events and forums that bring together women involved in heritage preservation and promotion to exchange ideas and experiences, providing support and resources to businesswomen working in heritage tourism, establishing research networks that encourage collaboration and sharing of information among academicians and researchers and encouraging the media coverage of heritage-related events.

As for the Buddhist heritage of the region, developing trails that connect important sites across the region can showcase the diversity of this heritage and encourage visitors to participate in rituals and ceremonies and experience the spiritual aspects of this expertise in different member countries. Initiatives such as establishing a heritage fund, cultural heritage networks and developing cultural exchange programmes can also be considered. These programmes could include exhibitions, performances and other cultural activities.

The region boasts some of the world's most iconic architectural structures, ranging from ancient temples to modern skyscrapers. It is crucial to support the preservation and promotion of these important sites by designating them as Heritage Sites and establishing an Architecture Heritage Fund. This would not only help preserve these sites, but also highlight their significance and promote them to a wider audience.

The region has a rich literary tradition, spanning across several centuries. Creating a Literary Translation Project to promote the translation of the important literary works of the different SCO countries into other languages as well as literary awards and festivals can increase awareness and encourage greater appreciation for the diversity of the region. The SCO member countries have produced some of the greatest thinkers, scientists, philosophers and inventors in history.

By creating an SCO Personalities Museum, we can inspire the future generations and foster a greater sense of pride towards heritage, while developing the tourism infrastructure around these sites to ensure a convenient experience.

The Kingdom of Bahrain is committed to collaborate with the SCO and its member states to promote greater prosperity in our region. The challenges we face as a global community are significant, yet, together we can create a future of peace and shared success.

11

Why does the Shanghai Cooperation Organisation Matter to Egypt?

Ahmed Kandil

On September 14, 2022, Egypt signed a memorandum of understanding on its association with the SCO as a dialogue partner. This was an important step towards strengthening Cairo's relations with the SCO countries in several fields, such as trade, investment, energy, tourism, transport, agriculture, information and communication technology and cybersecurity as well as supporting regional security and stability.

Established in 2001 as a successor to the Shanghai Five, the SCO is the largest regional organisation in the world, covering more than half of its population and 30% of its economic output. Owing to its impressive profile of security and economic cooperation, the SCO has gained enormous traction in Egypt. Enhancing relations with the SCO countries will likely help Cairo to achieve its national interests. Since February 2016, Egypt has adopted comprehensive reforms implemented within the framework of "Egypt's Vision 2030 to achieve sustainable development goals". It has also adopted several social programmes such as "Solidarity and Dignity" and "Decent Life" as well as initiatives aimed at reducing poverty and attracting foreign investment. Cooperation with the SCO countries will likely contribute significantly in the successful implementation of such initiatives and programmes.

Egypt's accession to the SCO is also being seen as part of the government's push to engage the 'Global South' and as a rekindling of the principles of non-alignment that have returned to the fore after the Russian war in Ukraine began in February 2022. In this context, we, the Egyptians, have deep cultural and civilisational ties with most SCO peoples as well as having common principles of non-intervention, respect of sovereignty and no use of force. Furthermore, Egypt and the SCO are finding more and more in common in a world where the need for strategic autonomy is replacing many traditional alliances in the developing world.

By joining the SCO, Egypt aims to diversify its partners. The negative repercussions of the Russian-Ukrainian war, especially on food security and energy, have served to reinforce the importance of 'diversifying allies' in order to strengthen stability at home. For example, increasing the number of national currencies used in mutual settlements and providing alternatives to the dollar or euro can only be of benefit to Egypt, where hard currency reserves are under pressure from current economic conditions.

In addition, Egypt is a vital partner of the SCO. With a population of almost 105 million, a location that straddles Africa and Asia, a standing army that is the largest in the region, a capital that hosts the League of Arab States and a diplomatic presence that punches above its weight in global affairs, Egypt is a pivotal player to achieve the SCO's objectives. Our partnership will likely contribute to peace and stability in Central Asia, North Africa and West Asia, including in counter-terrorism and the prevention of violent extremism. Security measures are vital, but they are just one part of the solution. Egypt can work with the SCO countries to support holistic efforts to prevent and counter terrorism by dealing with root causes, with full respect for the rule of law and human rights.

However, our cooperation goes far beyond counter-terrorism. The commitment of the SCO to developing joint solutions to shared challenges is all the more significant today, as the world faces pressing, interconnected crises. Food insecurity, poverty and climate change are being exacerbated by the global financial and economic turmoil.

The partnership between Egypt and the SCO will further the collective efforts of the international community in responding to energy crises, climate change, food shortages, scarcity of financing for development and the accumulation of debts owed by developing countries. These are issues that we place on the top of our priorities, in an effort to restore stability and balance to the international economic environment.

For this reason, we, in Egypt, support strengthening interactions between Egypt and regional organisations, including the SCO. The need for enhanced collaboration with regional organisations was a strong message delivered by COP27, held in Sharm El Sheikh, in November 2022, to deal with climate change. The climate crisis, like the pandemic, is a global threat that knows no borders. With more than 110 countries having committed to net zero emissions by 2050 and China, before 2060, Egypt and the SCO have great opportunities to cooperate on issues of climate adaptation, combating desertification and ways to enhance reliance on renewable energy, including Green Hydrogen. This could be supported by COP27's establishment of the 'Loss and Damage Fund' to help developing countries exposed to the negative effects of climate change.

Egypt's dialogue partner status in the SCO had been on the cards for years, but its implementation had been delayed due to the COVID-19 pandemic. Cairo remained sensitive about full membership of the grouping, lest it be viewed in the West as a hostile move, especially given the current anti-China and anti-Russia mood in Washington. The SCO was also initially branded by the US as a hostile bloc, led by China and Russia, to challenge its post-Cold War global supremacy. Quite the contrary, its evolution conforms to the familiar pattern of 'new regionalism' in the developing world. The strategic mission of the SCO makes it the best option for Egypt as it seeks to diversify geoeconomic linkages in Asia, without jeopardising its geopolitical partnership with the US. These two paths are not at cross-purposes, as one ensures economic prosperity and the other provides security guarantee.

Together with Saudi Arabia, the UAE and other Arabian aspirants of SCO partnership, Egypt has the wherewithal to act as a catalyst in Eurasian regionalism, along with India, China, Russia and the resource-rich Central Asian and Caucasus members.

Egypt, no doubt, is a late entrant in this pivotal regional body. However, better late than never. In fact, Egypt can use its formidable political, geographic and economic clout to shape the SCO's progressive agenda in its own way. In this regard, Egypt can share its exceptional expertise in many fields, such as renewable energy, with the SCO. In joining our efforts, Egypt and the SCO can make a positive contribution to the lives of people in Eurasia, North Africa and West Asia, thus strengthening regional cooperation at all levels. Together, we can seize today's opportunities for progress.

12

Shanghai Cooperation Organisation: Significance and Cambodia's Engagement

Lim Menghour

Introduction

The demise of the Soviet Union marked the largest transformation of geopolitics in Central Asia, with the birth of five newly independent states, namely, Kazakhstan, Kyrgyzstan, Tajikistan, Turkmenistan and Uzbekistan, lumped together as 'the Stans'. However, it also brought catastrophe to the region as the retreat of the communist ideology enabled Islamism to take a centre stage and defined the regional security agenda, while border disputes loomed large among the new nation-states. Chaos, instability and insecurity reign, with serious ramifications for not only the newly independent states, but also the regional powers.

For China, the emergence of the newly independent states along its western flank might exemplarily provoke the secessionist movement among the ethnic Uyghurs in the Xinjiang region, with the infiltration of radical Islam from the region. Maintaining good relations with the post-Soviet states, therefore, played to its advantage. As for Russia, it was alarmed not only by the terrorist attacks and separatism in its territory, but also NATO's ongoing eastward expansion and its military intervention in the 1999 Kosovo War, which the Kremlin viewed as existential threats to its regime and influence in its "near abroad".

For Central Asian countries, ensuring regime survival and stability were first and foremost. These security concerns led to the rise of a regional mechanism, the so-called 'Shanghai Five' (China, Russia, Kazakhstan, Kyrgyzstan and Tajikistan) in 1996, which was later transformed into 'The Shanghai Cooperation Organisation (SCO)' in June 2001 to include Uzbekistan as a core member. The full member states of the SCO have expanded to include India and Pakistan in 2017 as well as Iran in 2022, taking the tally of full member states to nine. Besides, the SCO has three observers (Afghanistan, Belarus and Mongolia) and six dialogue partners (Azerbaijan, Armenia, Cambodia, Nepal, Sri Lanka and Turkey). The 2022 SCO Summit, which took place in Samarkand, Uzbekistan, in September, agreed on the further expansion of its organisation and announced Iran's full membership. It also approved the request for full membership by Belarus and the requests of Bahrain, Myanmar, the UAE, Kuwait, Egypt, Qatar, Saudi Arabia and Maldives to become dialogue partners.

Over time, the scope of cooperation under this framework has been expanded to cover a broad range of issues, including:

- strengthening mutual trust, friendship and good neighbourliness;
- consolidating multi-disciplinary cooperation in regional peace, security and stability;
- promoting a new democratic, fair and rational political and economic international order;
- jointly counteracting terrorism, separatism and extremism, illicit narcotics and arms trafficking;
- encouraging efficient regional cooperation in such spheres as politics, trade and economy, defence, law enforcement, environmental protection, culture, science and technology, education, energy, transport, credit and finance (Charter of the SCO).

The SCO has been incrementally institutionalised through the creation of its Charter in 2002. The SCO Secretariat and its Regional Anti-Terrorist Structure (RATS) are based in Beijing and in the Uzbekistan capital city of Tashkent, respectively. Other specialised SCO bodies, including the SCO Business Council, the Interbank Consortium, the University network and the SCO Energy Club have also been subsequently established. Like ASEAN, all decisions are passed by consensus. Member states can opt out of any resolution if it does not serve their interests. However, they are free to join at a later stage. Non-interference in the internal affairs of other states constitutes the SCO's fundamental principle. The SCO's highest body is the Council of Heads of State, which is chaired annually by the host of the upcoming summit.

The SCO is the world's largest regional organisation, covering around 40 percent of the world's population and more than 30 percent of the global GDP (*NDTV*, 2022). The organisation aims to achieve its goals by strengthening mutual trust, friendship and good neighbourliness between its members. Its primary areas of cooperation include the fight against terrorism, separatism, extremism, arms trafficking, illegal immigration and other types of criminal activities of a transnational nature. The SCO also aims to promote regional connectivity, energy systems and cooperation in science, technology, education, health care, culture, sports and tourism. The SCO and its members adhere to a set of principles, which include mutual respect for the sovereignty, independence and territorial integrity of states and the inviolability of state borders, non-aggression, non-interference in internal affairs, non-use of force or threat of its use in international relations and seeking no unilateral superiority in the region (Charter of the SCO).

This paper will examine: (1) the significant role of the SCO in promoting regional and global development, (2) Cambodia's engagement in the SCO and (3) the ways forward for the SCO.

Why Does The SCO Matter?

Without a doubt, under the framework of the SCO, the region becomes a new development frontier. Under its founding Charter, the SCO supports and promotes regional economic cooperation in various forms, thus fostering a favourable environment for trade and investments. This would require the modernisation of communication and infrastructure development to ensure the free flow of trade and other economic activities. For instance, transport corridors, such as air, rail and road have been developed to create a criss-crossed network among the member countries. Cooperation in the energy sector has also rapidly progressed.

Economically, the SCO members benefit from enhanced trade and commercial dealings, broader access to commodities and the improvement of national and regional infrastructure for transport and communication within the organisation.

The SCO adopted the Development Strategy (2015-2025) during the Ufa Summit, in Russia, in June 2015, to boost cooperation in finance, investment and trade. The Ufa Development Strategy has allowed China to promote its cross-border energy trade with other SCO member states and investment in them. For China, the strategy would help to materialise its Belt and Road Initiative (BRI) and simultaneously, serve as an alternative to sea route for both goods and more importantly, energy flows from and across the region, thereby reducing the risks stemming from the potential cut-off, especially at the Strait of Malacca (Ventura Jariod & Martinez de Oses, 2020).

Among others, Russia has considered the SCO as a viable platform to seek economic opportunities from China, amidst economic pressures from the West, following the annexation of Crimea in 2014. Other members are interested in developing infrastructure, energy and tourism sectors. India and Pakistan are also involved, one way or another, in regional energy ventures, particularly the development of gas pipelines. For the landlocked Central Asian countries, infrastructure development is crucial for them to access regional markets and seaports.

However, most member states, particularly, Russia and the Central Asian countries, remain wary of China's economic predominance. Indeed, China has already overtaken Russia as Central Asia's leading trade partner (*The Economist*, 2023). This has potentially constrained the idea of the development of SCO's Free Trade Area. Moreover, given the existing rift between China and India, the free trade agenda, strongly favoured by China, will be put on the back burner, in the foreseeable future.

Politically, the SCO contributes to enhancing political stability and regime legitimacy of the member states through the socialisation and internalisation of the non-interference norms and respect for different national development paths. This was epitomised by the Tulip Revolution in Kyrgyzstan and Uzbekistan's uprising in 2005. On the regional level, the SCO is an essential platform where the member states can voice their concerns and collectively hedge against the pressures from the West.

Apart from the security and stability that the SCO's member states commonly share, the SCO serves a number of similar, yet, differentiated strategic interests. For China, the SCO is, to a large extent, the cornerstone of its regional policy to increase its influence in the region (Yuan, 2022). Unlike China, the SCO is not the only regional framework that plays a crucial role in Russia's Central Asia strategy. Russia exerts its influence through the SCO, the Russia-led Collective Security Treaty Organisation (CSTO) and the Eurasian Economic Union. Moreover, Russia still maintains its bilateral military dominance in the region and would, therefore, be reluctant to support the SCO develop into the mechanism that increases the military role of other member states in the region (Christoffersen, 2022).

For India and Pakistan, despite their interests in security and energy supply, the SCO is vital for their foreign policy thinkers for different reasons. Similarly, the SCO is a convenient platform for their engagement with regional powers. However, as India wants to be one of Asia's leading powers, it cannot be overshadowed by China. For Pakistan, the SCO offers another political privilege to deepen its relationship with both Russia and China. From the perspective of the Central Asian states, they are not merely recipients of periodic doses of foreign aid, but through the SCO, they can exert greater influence in shaping regional norms and agendas and therefore, alleviate their fear that they are being crowded out by Russia and China.

Cambodia's Engagement with the SCO

It is increasingly clear that the SCO will play an increasingly fundamental role in Central Asia and beyond in the years to come. As a SCO dialogue partner since 2015, Cambodia has seen tremendous potential for promoting comprehensive cooperation with the organisation, which will bolster its socio-economic development and shape the opportunity for export diversification. Cambodia has strongly supported the objectives and principles of the SCO. In July 2017, Cambodia officially requested to upgrade its engagement in the SCO to an observer status.

Economically, Cambodia will be able to capitalise on the economic opportunities stemming from this regional grouping. This would serve to realise the objective of Cambodia's economic diplomacy and diversification strategy. Such massive economies present a raft of tremendous opportunities through specific areas of cooperation for Cambodia, including the energy sector and agricultural products in the region.

Politically, the SCO provides a platform to increase the regime legitimacy of the government, especially in countering the diplomatic, political and economic pressures from the West. For instance, in 2018, the election observers from the SCO fully endorsed the results of the elections held in Cambodia. Receiving such a kind of political buttress enhanced the legitimacy of Cambodia, regionally and internationally.

Geopolitically, Cambodia's active engagement with the SCO can leverage its international standing. Cambodia can use this platform to articulate its foreign policy agenda and shape international norms and rules that serve its national interests. Expanding networks of strategic partners, promoting multilateralism for shared prosperity and enhancing the international norms of non-interference are part and parcel of Cambodia's foreign policy objectives and interests.

As Asia becomes a battleground for the rivalry between China and the US, Cambodia would be under immense pressure to carefully navigate her foreign policy moving forward. As such, since the SCO reaffirms the principle of neutrality and the right of peoples to independently and democratically choose their political and socio-economic developments, it also benefits Cambodia's foreign policy of non-alignment.

Ways Forward

In the fast changing, uncertain and complex scenario that our world is facing, we cannot afford to turn our back on multilateralism, if we are to genuinely address the common challenges of our times. In this connection, the SCO and the rest of the international community need to double down on efforts to revitalise multilateralism that gives priority to convergence in addressing challenges.

Over the recent decades, multilateralism has proven to be the driving force for the international community to cooperate in a mutually beneficial manner to address both challenges and matters of shared concerns. The global outbreak of the COVID-19 pandemic is testimony to the same. The war against this disease can only be won if countries across the globe join hands in solidarity and no single country could unilaterally and effectively address the negative impacts arising from this unprecedented global health crisis and other global issues that are trans-boundary in nature.

However, multilateralism is currently facing contention with increasing complexity and uncertainty due to the persistence and accentuation of regional tensions, zero-sum power competitions, reactionary populism, development gaps and non-traditional security threats, such as climate change and pandemics as well as the anti-multilateralism sentiment, such as unilateralism, de-globalisation, protectionism and isolationism. These pervasive challenges are threatening and weakening the progress of multilateralism, which has been playing a crucial role in promoting peace, stability and prosperity in the region and the world at large.

Cambodia, like many other countries, is of the view that multilateralism is the core global mechanism that needs to be strengthened and revitalised in order to enhance cross-border cooperation and coordination within the region and beyond, to address the current issues and prepare for the future ones. Hosting the 13th Asia-Europe Meeting (ASEM13) under the theme "Strengthening Multilateralism for Shared Growth", leaders reaffirmed the importance of this partnership between Asia and Europe in strengthening dialogue and fostering action-oriented cooperation, based on consensus, equal partnership, mutual respect and mutual benefit, to further advance a robust, inclusive and open multilateralism, which is capable of addressing global and regional issues.

To contribute to international peace and prosperity through international cooperation and integration, Cambodia is honoured and privileged to steer ASEAN's community building and external relations for the third time, as the ASEAN's Chair, in 2022. Under the theme of "ASEAN A.T.C.: Addressing Challenges Together", Cambodia stresses action-oriented and results-based regional cooperation to add our stone to the building of a harmonious ASEAN community that is peaceful, stable and prosperous, strengthening ASEAN's engagement with the wider region and developing regional responses to the impacts and uncertainties posed by regional and global challenges.

As it is the only country in ASEAN that holds a dialogue partner status in the SCO, Cambodia could act as a bridge to promote cooperation between ASEAN and the SCO, thereby promoting the exchange of experiences and knowledge on peace and mediation, the fight against terrorism and violent extremism and transnational organised crimes.

At the same time, we need to continue attaching great importance to the rules-based international system, with the United Nations at its core, which enables cooperation rather than confrontation, to be promoted. Moreover, countries should not be hindered by the imposition of unilateral sanctions, economic embargoes or other coercive measures that violate international law and the core principles and purposes, enshrined in the United Nations Charter.

Cambodia has recently worked on a concept note for the creation of a 'Universal Peace Charter', driven by the six interconnected core principles of peaceful coexistence, mutual respect, tolerance, unity in diversity, non-interference and peaceful settlement of disputes and differences. This Universal Peace Charter thus embraces the faith of the United Nations in promoting peace, tolerance and sustainable development in the context of a complex new world order, characterised by conflicts between societies and nations.

Regarding the post-COVID-19 recovery in an inclusive, sustainable and resilient manner, it is also imperative for us to work closely together to ensure that we are on the right track to achieve the 2030 UN Sustainable Development Goals (SDGs). In this regard, it is important to focus on all initiatives that involve international cooperation and efforts to support the less developed countries, especially those that the pandemic hit particularly hard. In this connection, the SCO should continue to focus on the promotion of people-centred building. It must be both a top-down regionalism and bottom-up regionalisation in its march towards the next decades.

Conclusion

The SCO has become a new development frontier for its member states and the region. Economically, it allows the members to reap the benefits from enhanced trade and commercial dealings, broader access to commodities and the improvement of national and regional infrastructure for transport and communication within the organisation. Politically, the SCO contributes significantly to enhancing political stability and regime legitimacy of the member states through the socialisation and internalisation of the non-interference norms and respect for different national development paths.

Cambodia could capitalise on the economic opportunities arising from this regional grouping to realise its economic diplomacy and diversification strategy. The SCO also provides a platform for it to increase the regime legitimacy internationally. In addition, Cambodia could use this platform to articulate its foreign policy agenda and shape international norms and rules that serve the country's national interest.

As a way forward, the SCO needs to further promote efforts to revitalise multilateralism that will give priority to convergence in addressing the challenges that we are facing in our times. In this connection, it is also vital to attach great importance to the rules-based international system, with the United Nations at its core, which enables cooperation rather than confrontation.

References

Charter of the Shanghai Cooperation Organization. Available online at: https://www.iri.edu.ar/publicaciones_iri/manual/Doc.%20Manual/Listos%20para%20subir/ASIA/SHANGAI-ORG/charter_shanghai_cooperation_organization.pdf

Christoffersen, G. (2022). 'Central Asia Over a Decade: The Shifting Balance in Central Asia Between Russia and China.' *International Politics, Johns Hopkins University, SAIS.* Available online at: https://theasanforum.org/central-asia-over-a-decade-the-shifting-balance-in-central-asia-between-russia-and-china/

NDTV (2022). 'The Big SCO Summit with PM Modi, Xi Jinping, Vladimir Putin: 10-Point Guide.' Available online at: https://www.ndtv.com/world-news/the-big-sco-summit-with-pm-modi-xi-jinping-vladimir-putin-10-point-guide-3337073

The Economist (2023). 'China and Russia Compete for Central Asia's Favour.' Available online at: https://www.economist.com/finance-and-economics/2023/05/25/china-and-russia-compete-for-central-asias-favour

Ventura Jariod, E., & Martinez de Oses, F.X. (2020). 'The Role of the Malacca Strait in the One Belt, One Road Initiative.' *Proceedings of the 8th International Conference on Maritime Transport: Technology, Innovation and Research.* Available online at: https://upcommons.upc.edu/bitstream/handle/2117/329696/05_Ventura.pdf

Yuan, J. (2022). 'Forging a New Security Order in Eurasia: China, the SCO and the Impacts on Regional Governance.', *China Political Science Review,* Available online at: https://doi.org/10.1007/s41111-022-00223-7

13

Reconnect for Stability: Ensuring Secure Re-Emergence of Eurasia

Jasem Al-Najem

Over the past 22 years, since its formation, the SCO has made important contributions to the peace and stability, development and prosperity of countries, especially at a time when the global trend is shifting towards the SCO region. In this context, the SCO has grown into an important platform for regional cooperation on the Eurasian continent.

The regional and global scenarios are undergoing deep and complex changes, which have profound implications in political, security, economic and other spheres. Upholding peace and pursuing development remain the trend of our times and the people's aspirations.

With this in mind, we need to work together to boost the 'Shanghai Spirit' and to safeguard security and stability for the betterment of all countries.

In order to provide enhanced stability to Eurasia and the SCO region, our cooperation mechanisms between the competent authorities must focus on tackling security threats, including counter-terrorism and its financing, drug and human trafficking, money laundering and cross-border organised crimes.

We need to expand security cooperation and build balanced, effective and sustainable security architecture in order to eliminate the threat of terrorism, separatism and extremism.

The induction of the Arab and Gulf countries as dialogue partners of the SCO signifies the growing importance of this platform in the Middle East and underlines the desire to play a greater role in developing cooperation among the Asian countries as well.

Kuwait remained an active member of the Global Coalition to Defeat terror groups, participating in a number of ministerial-level meetings throughout the year. Kuwait has also long been an active member of the Arab League, the Organisation of Islamic Cooperation and other international organisations engaged in counter-terrorism cooperation.

The situation in Afghanistan remains a major concern for the region. The Afghan people require support and concerted action. The SCO states have already assumed great responsibility in this regard.

In view of the evolving humanitarian situation in Afghanistan, Kuwait supports continued efforts to help the Afghan people achieve their aspirations and basic needs. It is also committed to work with international and regional groups to provide aid and humanitarian relief to the Afghan people.

Expanding cultural interactions within the SCO region, promoting mutual understanding among its peoples and respecting their cultural traditions and customs and preserving and enhancing cultural diversity within the SCO space will remain a high priority for our work, aimed at promoting peace, security and sustainable development.

These critical goals can be achieved through the promotion of cultural exchanges and cooperation between the countries of the region. The spirit of solidarity and cooperation will continue to guide the SCO as we work to advance peace and security, sustainable development and human rights.

14

Perspective on the SCO from Maldives

Aly Shameem

We extend our profound appreciation to the host and organisers of this conference for inviting the environmentally endangered, developing small island-state of Maldives to be represented at this important platform and have its voice heard. Indeed, we are very grateful to the host and the organisers for inviting the Maldives, which happens to be the smallest state present here. Oftentimes, due to the small size of our country, the organisers of such events would forget us in the past, until the Maldives came into the limelight as the most sought-after tourist destination in the Indian Ocean.

The Maldives has been profiled in the climate change discourse as an experimental laboratory in the face of global warming, since it is the lowest lying nation above sea level. By inviting the Maldives, the host and the organisers have truly honoured the founding principle of the SCO, which is the sovereign equality of all states. We, the Maldivians, believe in the principle of universality, just like a jungle becomes a true jungle when the smallest species and the largest elephants live in harmony as its stakeholders. Similarly, an ocean becomes a real ocean when the smallest species live with the largest whales to create the marine ecosystem. Therefore, the international community would be incomplete if small, medium and large nations could not interact and coexist in harmony.

The theme, 'Reconnecting the People: Invigorating Hearts & Minds', is the most touching and rewarding theme for reconnecting and rejuvenating the people of the Shanghai Cooperation Organisation and those of like-minded countries, such as the Maldives.

Indeed, today, no agenda of any international conference could be complete without the most sought-after goals of the world, namely, sustaining peace and prompting sustainable development. It has been long recognised that understanding cultural diversity to appreciate differences and tolerance towards each other are indispensable for sustaining peace. Nevertheless, the goals of the promotion of understanding of cultural diversity and people-to-people connectivity have been mentioned again and again in the documents, but when they are being addressed for implementation, they receive neither political will nor adequate finances nor priority. Subsequently, these matters are relegated to the lowest line of the agenda or plan.

Therefore, it may be appealed through this platform to make a concrete commitment this time to facilitate cultural dialogue and the promotion of understanding towards diversity. People-to-people connectivity is crucial for this process, along with educating communities to that effect.

An impediment to people-to-people connectivity is the disfavoured practice of international differential fees, charged by many countries, to foreign nationals for university studies and medical services. The Maldivians regard the levying of international differential fees for foreign students and foreign patients as an unfair practice. As for the Maldives, we have foreign diaspora close to half of the population in the country, but we do not charge extra fees for foreign students or foreign patients. It is our conviction that there must be reciprocal treatment at the least.

Perhaps, this is a matter that the SCO can put on its agenda and negotiate for a solution that could facilitate greater people-to-people connectivity, by removing the barrier of international deferential fees.

A personal experience from a fruitful programme recently completed in Greece can be shared. The author was nominated by his university to undertake the International Mobility Exchange Programme, organised by the member universities of the European Union and funded by the European Union. A visit to a Greek university called the University of Aegean was made for the week-long training programme and exposure to the Greek culture and expertise in teaching excellence and quality assurance that the university had achieved. The author was quite refreshed and had upgraded his skills through this programme. He began to teach and practice what he had learned from this programme in his university immediately. Reciprocally, a researcher from the Greek university visited a university in the Maldives to learn about the culture of the Maldives and gain exposure to research activities at the Maldives National University. This programme is definitely very fruitful and mutually beneficial to achieve people-to-people contact. If the SCO authorities could arrange such a programme, it would greatly facilitate inter-cultural dialogue and understanding.

It is suggested that an eminent commission be constituted by the SCO to develop a curriculum and teaching materials for teaching at member universities to promote cultural diversity and tolerance towards differences. The deliberations that have taken place at this conference could be summarised as topics to be covered in this SCO curriculum.

The author would like to cite another success story from the United Arab Emirates, where a successful programme is being run to cultivate a culture of happiness among its citizens:

- The UAE was the first country to appoint a Minister for Happiness and Tolerance.
- The UAE has a programme running nationwide on happiness, positivity, tolerance and values.
- About 60 Chief Officers work in the UAE to promote happiness by institutionalising the concept, disseminating information and monitoring progress.
- There are also Happiness Champions appointed in the UAE, who promote happiness in the country.
- Three levels were identified to promote the concept: (i) Employee level (ii) Customers level and (iii) School level.
- About 1,16,000 students were trained in the UAE schools to educate minds and hearts, in order to influence families and parents.
- 100 Days of Positivity were observed in the UAE schools every year.
- Conducting some dialogue sessions among the UAE citizens and migrant workers, surveys and the collection of data helped to measure happiness, well-being and sustainability and also assisted in developing further happiness policies and programmes.
- It was observed that countries can no longer rely on the assumption that ever-increasing economic growth and consumption will lead to greater happiness for people.

Perhaps, we could give some thought to this case study from the UAE as a model for reconnecting people and invigorating hearts and minds.

If we could agree on a concrete action to be taken immediately for connecting the people and invigorating their hearts and minds, an ideal first step would be to observe or mark a 'SCO Day' or 'International Day' annually in SCO countries, observer states and dialogue partners.

Another important area is to connect the younger generation and make them aware of the rich heritage of the SCO region, in order to further strengthen mutual understanding. A question that haunts the consciousness may be asked - do the youth have access or the means to make a real impact on the national decision making process of our countries? Oftentimes, governments are criticised for marginalising the youth in the national decision-making processes or the youth being under-represented in decision-making bodies like parliaments and meetings of international organisations.

According to the world population statistics, 70 percent of the world's population is under 35 years of age, which means that the youth comprise two-third of the world's population. To reflect this reality in national and international decision-making processes or platforms, the youth can demand that they be included in representations of the national and state governments as well as international organisations.

A number of countries have set quotas for women candidates in parliaments and local councils. This is a very encouraging democratic development, but to be more democratic, the youth must also be allowed quotas in these institutions.

Another proposal for consideration is: could we agree to call on the authorities of the SCO member governments to set a quota in elected institutions and national delegations to include at least 5 percent of the youth representation in each country?

Unless we can institutionalise actions, this conference will be recorded as another routine event, which has not generated any tangible result. Undoubtedly and surely, the leadership of the Indian Council of World Affairs and Shanghai Cooperation Organisation will not let this conference be concluded on an empty note, but with a substantial call for concrete actions.

15

SCO: A Perspective from the UAE

Ebtesam Alteneiji

We live in a turbulent world with profound and complex developments, both regionally and internationally, which are driving heightened uncertainty, with destabilising effects. Stability is essential for sustainable economic growth and this is where connectivity is more important than ever before, elevating multilateral mechanisms like the SCO to an even greater level of significance.

Connectivity is a Great Enabler:

- In laying the foundations for stronger trade and investment ties, but perhaps more importantly, to build bridges of communication that help foster the common understanding needed to tackle trade bottlenecks and embrace opportunities.
- For the potential gains from deeper SCO cooperation, ranging from enhanced supply chain security and efficient resource utilisation to furthering joint efforts on environmental protection and greater digital and energy connectivity.
- Establishing a new model of regional cooperation, one that prioritises connectivity and development projects and is a constructive step forward in strengthening multilateral relations in Eurasia and beyond.
- Expanding the SCO to include the UAE as a dialogue partner is testament to the growing relevance of the organisation, but it also underscores the importance of regional connectivity and the natural synergies that exist in Southwest Asia.

The UAE's robust economy has significant potential for the SCO space, offering a range of proven competitive advantages through its strategic location, world-class smart logistics and transport infrastructure, multimodal connectivity corridors and free-trade agreements. These unique features, coupled with the UAE's extensive experience across these areas, enable connectivity and expand reach across the Middle East and North Africa as well as Asian markets.

The UAE's multilateral cooperation approach, focused on enhancing connectivity through a range of initiatives, has seen trade flows grow between the UAE and the members of the SCO over the years. For instance, China and India are the UAE's second and third largest trading partners respectively.

This growth in investment and trade connectivity reflects the scope of cooperation, which is no longer limited to traditional infrastructure, but includes new sectors, with the most promising synergies to be found in green energy, agriculture and smart logistics.

If we take a closer look at some of the key connectivity initiatives in the SCO space and areas where potential synergies could have a significant impact, climate action, agricultural development and digital connectivity stand out.

The UAE, being the host of COP28, along with many countries in the SCO space, has pledged to achieve carbon neutrality in the next 30-40 years. New regional synergies are emerging as climate action becomes important in global economic growth and big connectivity projects, such as the Belt and Road Initiative (BRI).

Within the BRI framework, one potential synergy is the development of the hydrogen supply chain, particularly green hydrogen. The potential of the green hydrogen market in the SCO space is immense. However, achieving its economic potential requires cost reduction by investing heavily in new technologies and new infrastructures as well as workforce training.

Another crucial collaborative area in the SCO space relates to securing food chains and agricultural development. The India-UAE Food Corridor initiative has the potential to become a replicable model for agri-synergy within the SCO space, harnessing combined commercial and technological strengths to:

- build a robust food supply chain,
- reduce waste by investing in mega food parks, warehouses and logistics
- and finally, alleviate poverty by creating additional local jobs.

There are opportunities for greater digital connectivity amongst countries in the SCO orbit, particularly in promoting smart infrastructure, paperless trade and intelligent transport and logistics. In many geographies, logistics still relies heavily on manual and paper-based processes, in which automation, Internet of Things (IoT) and block chains are still new. Therefore, investment in smart supply chain solutions is essential to loosen bottlenecks and unlock market access.

In the light of this, an exemplary initiative of the UAE, the World Logistics Passport (WLP) needs to be highlighted. It is the first multi-modal global freight loyalty scheme offering fast-tracking of cargo movement across borders, thereby reducing the administrative cost and advancing cargo information across borders. The WLP now has hubs in over 15 countries. India, China and Kazakhstan are already members of the WLP initiative.

In conclusion, greater SCO connectivity should be guided by three principles: anchoring decarbonisation, seeking greater resilience through multimodal corridors and leveraging digitisation.

16

Sri Lanka's Potential as a Leading Maritime Hub and Opportunities for Enhanced Connectivity amongst the SCO Member States

Yasoja Gunasekara

Abstract

Connectivity is a fundamental factor in enhancing trade, investment and commerce, people-to-people contact, energy, infrastructure and transport. From ancient times, Sri Lanka has been an important hub on the maritime trade routes and in that context, has relationships with many member states, observer states and dialogue partners of the SCO that go back centuries. Sri Lanka values its connectivity with friendly countries. In the modern context, this includes maritime, air, trade, energy and digital connectivity as well as people to people engagement. In the modern age, Sri Lanka is working towards using its unique locational advantage to become one of the world's leading maritime hubs. The Sri Lankan government's ultimate goal is to re-establish our past legacy to create a strong and developed green economy. As Sri Lanka transforms itself into an important financial, logistical and business hub, we hope that companies from the SCO region would consider setting up manufacturing and processing facilities in our country.

Sri Lanka, as a dialogue partner, welcomes the ongoing efforts to strengthen interconnectedness between Central and South Asia to contribute to achieving the common goal of prosperity and security in the SCO region through economic, transportation and communication ties. Sharing a land and maritime border, the SCO neighbours are connected through important economic, diplomatic and cultural ties dating back centuries. It is noted that cooperation through the SCO has the potential to enable smooth access to ports in maritime countries, such as Sri Lanka, to landlocked countries in the SCO region, in order to expand their trading networks, leading to enhanced prosperity for the whole region.

The trade and investment component of the SCO countries should be revitalised to stay relevant. It is imperative that we further strengthen our collaborative efforts to enhance intra-regional trade, focusing on our competitive advantages. The participation of the private sectors in the region and networking among them would be a significant step towards this end.

Sri Lanka's strategy toward fostering regional connectivity has included a focus on strengthening win-win economic cooperation with its neighbours in Asia. The world has become interconnected through modern information technology. We are living in a world of exciting technological innovations and these digital technologies have become the driving force in transforming the world we live in. Sri Lanka hopes that, with the establishment of regional digital engagement mechanisms, the access to opportunities for our countries to engage will be enhanced further.

Ultimately, the success of the SCO will be determined by its contributions to the economic growth and prosperity of the peoples of our countries. This region, bestowed with natural and human resources, vast lands and an abundance of ocean resources, is inherently dynamic.

Connectivity is a fundamental factor in enhancing trade, investment and commerce, people-to-people contact, energy, infrastructure and transport. Faster and more reliable inter-regional connectivity, including through ports and airports is vital for transporting goods and services.

From ancient times, Sri Lanka was known worldwide as a major economic hub located on the maritime trade routes. In the words of the Greek merchant and traveller, Cosmas Indicopleustes, the island served as the greatest emporium in those parts. Blessed with a rich endowment of natural harbours and ports as well as ship-building and nautical traditions, Sri Lanka was a meeting place of traders and their goods. It was well-known for its own trade products, which in the early days, included elephants, precious stones, pearls and spices. Further, Sri Lanka was identified as the 'Granary of the East'.

In the modern age, Sri Lanka is working towards using its unique locational advantage to become one of the world's leading maritime hubs. The Sri Lankan government's ultimate goal is to re-establish our past legacy to create a strong and developed green economy. This includes more investment in the logistics and transportation sectors, in order to play a significant role in facilitating regional supply chains as well as regional and global trade.

As Sri Lanka transforms itself into an important financial, logistical and business hub, we hope that companies from the Shanghai Cooperation Organisation region would consider setting up manufacturing and processing facilities in our country.

Sri Lankan President Ranil Wickremesinghe has stressed that before the end of the 21st century, the Asian region will be the most powerful economic domain in the world. In this context, the strategic geographical location of our country is extremely important and we are working towards making the best use of this favourable position.

Sri Lanka's Strategies Towards Regional Connectivity

The Shanghai Cooperation Organisation (SCO) is an important regional grouping through which member states and observers can engage towards mutual benefit. It is encouraging to note that countries from different parts of the world are seeking to become SCO partners. This meeting is an opportunity to hear the views of the SCO partners, both old and new, from diverse parts of the world and work towards identifying mechanisms for practical cooperation.

Most SCO member states see the SCO as holding untapped economic potential. The deliberations at the 2022 Shanghai Cooperation Organisation Summit, Samarkand, Uzbekistan, reflected an interest on the part of the SCO member states to transform the SCO into an organisation with clear economic and infrastructure-oriented goals. These goals include promoting new transportation routes, diversifying connectivity channels, securing the stability of supply chains and promoting wider opportunities for growth generation.

This is a good starting point from which to view the importance of enhanced connectivity in the SCO. The promotion of cooperation in transport, including the creation of new international routes and the modernisation of existing international routes for vehicles and railways, multimodal transport corridors and logistics centres has the potential to have a multiplier effect in terms of the economic growth of the region.

Sri Lanka, as a dialogue partner, welcomes the ongoing efforts to strengthen interconnectedness between Central and South Asia to contribute to achieving the common goal of prosperity and security in the SCO region through economic, transportation and communication ties. At the 22nd SCO Summit, the SCO leaders focused on the importance of new transit routes and economic cooperation. Sharing a land and maritime border, the SCO neighbours are connected through important economic, diplomatic and cultural ties dating back centuries.

It is noted that cooperation through the SCO has the potential to enable smooth access to ports in maritime countries, such as Sri Lanka, to landlocked countries in the SCO, in order to expand their trading networks, leading to enhanced prosperity for the whole region. Therefore, Sri Lanka is interested in working towards developing the Chabahar-Mumbai-Colombo shipping route, which will benefit the SCO member states.

The trade and investment component of the SCO countries should be revitalised to stay relevant. It is imperative that we further strengthen our collaborative efforts to enhance intra-regional trade, focusing on our competitive advantages. The participation of the private sectors in the region and networking among them would be a significant step towards this end. Sri Lanka's strategy towards fostering regional connectivity has included a focus on strengthening win-win economic cooperation with its neighbours in Asia. Since the mid-1990s, efforts have been made to gain market access and domestic export diversification through bilateral and regional preferential trade initiatives.

Furthermore, Sri Lanka is strengthening financial connectivity by establishing an offshore financial centre in the Colombo Port City.

The energy market of Sri Lanka mainly facilitates the exchange of electricity, petroleum and biomass. Some of the major energy sources, such as petroleum and coal, are fully imported. Switching to renewable energy resources is important for Sri Lanka to reduce its heavy reliance on imported fossil fuels and meet its growing energy demand.

Further, Sri Lanka has the potential for cross-border energy trade, primarily with its immediate neighbour, India.

The world has become interconnected through modern information technology. We are living in a world of exciting technological innovations and these digital technologies have become the driving force in transforming the world. The COVID-19 pandemic, in particular, accelerated technology penetration in every sector in countries around the world. The rising acceptance of e-commerce is an opportunity that is particularly worthy of being focused on, in terms of opportunities for regional connectivity.

Sri Lanka hopes that with the establishment of regional digital engagement mechanisms, the access to opportunities for our countries to engage will be enhanced further. Through investment in digital transformation, businesses can lay the foundation for long-term resilience to future crises and supply chains can improve long-term resilience.

Conclusion

Sri Lanka's geostrategic location as the nucleus of the Indian Ocean presents many opportunities to attract a diverse variety of nations and peoples. Over the centuries, from far and near, the region has seen many traders, seafarers, religious missionaries, scholars and writers on its shores.

Given the civilisational links that connect the SCO member states, the importance of people-to-people connectivity, including through travel, between our countries should be highlighted. Whilst the potential for cooperation goes beyond seeing each other as 'markets', the business communities in our countries could work towards exploring business opportunities, towards shared economic prosperity in our neighbourhood.

Sri Lanka's maritime heritage holds lessons of peaceful cooperation in trade and cultural exchanges. In the past, the maritime trade routes created mutual prosperity and exchange of ideas. In the future too, this common heritage can play an important role towards a peaceful and prosperous neighbourhood.

The success of this organisation will be determined by its contributions to the economic growth and the prosperity of the peoples of our countries. This region, bestowed with natural and human resources, vast lands and an abundance of ocean resources, is inherently dynamic.

Index